GRADE 6
Theory of Music
WORKBOOK

For Trinity College London
Theory of Music exams

by Naomi Yandell

Published by
Trinity College London Press Ltd
trinitycollege.com

Registered in England
Company no. 09726123

© Copyright 2025 Trinity College London Press Ltd
First impression, November 2025

Unauthorised photocopying is illegal
No part of this publication may be copied or reproduced in any
form or by any means without the prior permission of the publisher.

Cover artwork: Rod Steele
Printed in England by Caligraving Ltd

Grade 6 Theory of Music Syllabus from 2009

Section 1	10 questions	(10 marks)
Section 2	Writing scales, arpeggios, broken chords, transposition	(15 marks)
Section 3	Writing an 8-bar melody (using notes from major, minor, pentatonic major, pentatonic minor or blues scales or from the Aeolian mode). Clef, time signature, instrument and tonality are prescribed and an optional start is given	(15 marks)
Section 4	Harmonic sequence	(15 marks)
Section 5	4-part chords for SATB or transferring a short extract of a hymn/chorale from close to open score or vice versa	(10 marks)
Section 6	Labelling the chords of a phrase of a hymn/chorale with Roman numerals and chord symbols and completing it with an appropriate two-chord cadence (bass line given)	(15 marks)
Section 7	Analysis – 10 questions	(20 marks)

Questions and tasks may cover all matters specified in previous grades and also the following:

Rhythm, texture and form

1. Demisemiquaver triplets
2. Double dotted notes and rests
3. Duplets
4. Hemiola
5. Swung quavers (writing quavers to be played **swing**)
6. Understand and identify textures (homophonic, polyphonic, imitative, thick or dense, thin or transparent)
7. Understand the terms **movement** and **Prelude**
8. Binary form with reference particularly to Baroque sonatas (**da camera** and **da chiesa**) and dance suites (Allemande, Bourrée, Italian Corrente, French Courante, Italian Giga, French Gigue, Gavotte, Minuet and Sarabande – definitions for each as defined in the workbook)
9. Ternary form with reference particularly to Baroque dance suites (Bourrée I and II, Gavotte I and II and Minuet and Trio)
10. Air with variations
11. Chorale
12. Folk ballad

Composers

Composers of particular relevance to this grade are those writing in the Baroque period (approximately 1600-1750) eg J S Bach, Corelli, Couperin, Handel, Marcello, Rameau, A and D Scarlatti, Telemann and Vivaldi

Pitch

1. All major keys (for all major keys: scales, key signatures, arpeggios, broken chords, broken chords of the dominant 7th, and tonic triads (root, first or second inversion))
2. All minor keys (for all minor keys: scales – natural (Aeolian mode) and harmonic and melodic minor, key signatures, arpeggios, broken chords, broken chords of the dominant 7th, and tonic triads (root, first or second inversion))
3. 3rd, 6th and 7th degrees of the major/minor scale being known as mediant, submediant and leading note respectively
4. Recognising and writing diminished 7th chords (with an understanding of correct spelling and their enharmonic equivalents)
5. Broken chords of all diminished 7th chords

6. Writing and labelling chords on every degree of the scale (harmonic and melodic minors) in any key as well-balanced 4-part chords for SATB in root, first or second inversions (plus third inversions for dominant 7ths and diminished 7ths), using Roman numerals or chord symbols
7. Recognising and writing figured bass for all major and minor chords for the grade in root, first or second inversion
8. Recognising and writing augmented chords
9. Recognition of all intervals including compound intervals
10. Recognising pedal points on the tonic and dominant degrees of the scale
11. Recognising and writing harmonic sequences and identifying the keys that they travel through
12. Recognising and writing perfect, plagal, imperfect and interrupted cadences
13. Labelling the chords of a phrase of a chorale/hymn in Roman numerals and chord symbols, and completing it with an appropriate two-chord cadence (bass line given)
14. Writing a short extract from close to open score for SATB (chorale/hymn phrase), or vice versa
15. Recognising and writing C, D, F or G pentatonic major scales, A, B, D or E pentatonic minor and A, B, D or E blues scales
16. Concept of modes with reference particularly to Aeolian mode (the natural minor)
17. Identifying music written using the Aeolian mode (natural minor)
18. Writing an 8-bar melody using notes from the major, minor, pentatonic major, pentatonic minor, blues scales or using notes from the Aeolian mode
19. Transposing a melody for any transposing instrument for the grade (transposing interval to be known for descant recorder, clarinet in B♭, alto saxophone in E♭, tenor saxophone in B♭, trumpet in B♭, French horn in F, double bass and classical guitar)
20. Ranges of clarinet in A, treble recorder, saxophones (tenor in B♭ and baritone in E♭) as defined in the workbook
21. Identifying variation/decoration (harmonic, melodic, dynamic and textural)

General knowledge
Baroque period as defined in the workbook

Musical words and symbols
Instrument-specific words (bowed strings)
Arco, con sordino, natural harmonics, open strings, *pizz.*, double stopping, chords
Instrument names/terms in Italian
Basso continuo (or *continuo*), *contrabasso, corno, fagotto, flauto, flauto dolce, oboe, tromba, viola, violino, violoncello*

Please refer to the Theory Syllabus for details on all sections of the exam.
Check trinitycollege.com/theory to make sure you are using the current version.

Contents

Introduction 6	Figured bass 45
Note values and rests 8	4-part chords 47
Scales and melody writing 18	Close and open scores 49
Modes 25	Cadences 52
Working out the key or mode of a piece ... 26	Writing 4-part cadences for SATB 56
The circle of 5ths 29	Harmonic sequences 58
More about the new key signatures for Grade 6 ... 30	Texture 63
Arpeggios 33	Musical words and symbols 65
Transposing melodies 34	Analysis 73
Mediant, submediant and leading note triads ... 36	Sample examination paper 80
Broken chords – dominant 7ths 39	Instrument ranges 87
Diminished 7ths 40	Voice ranges 88
Broken chords – diminished 7ths 41	Different words – same meaning 88
Compound intervals 43	English and Italian words for instruments ... 88

Acknowledgements

Trinity College London would like to acknowledge the invaluable contribution to the development of this music theory programme by music teachers, professors, examiners, language specialists and students from around the world. Their comments have usefully informed the final shape of the workbooks and exam papers, and are much appreciated.

Introduction

Why write down music?

If you read a book you are reading another person's thoughts. If you play music you are playing another person's **musical** thoughts. People write books and music so that they can share their ideas.

Learning to read and write music is important because it helps musicians to play what is written down quickly and easily. Having said that, some brilliant musicians have never learned to read music. They play by ear. That's great, but if you want to play in bands and orchestras, or to write your own music, you need to learn to read and write music.

Using this workbook

Information in these boxes tells you:

- About the music that you sing, or play on your instrument
- What you need to know to pass your Trinity College London Theory of Music exam. Topics from the previous grade should also be known
- Important words or concepts are highlighted in pink

Handy tip!
These add additional insight into topics being covered.

Did you know?
These often contain extra interesting information.

Remember
Information in these boxes is a reminder of something previously covered.

 The pencil icon lets you know there are some exercises to fill in. For corrections, it is advisable to use a 'kneadable' eraser (also known as a putty rubber) as it will leave less of a smudge.

 01 The audio icon and track number are shown when there is accompanying audio to download (see inside back cover for more details).

 **Playlist:**

- Playlists are included to deepen understanding
- Either scan the QR code, or search for the piece online

6

Doing the tasks

- Use a pencil with a sharp point and a fairly soft lead so that you can easily rub out what you have written if you need to
- Be careful to be accurate with musical notes and signs – this will make a difference to your marks because written music needs to be clear for someone else to read or play
- Read through the boxes to make sure you understand how to do the tasks and ask for help if you need it
- The first task in each section has usually been done for you in **pink** to show you what to do
- Use the pictures of the piano keyboards, including the one on page 88. They are there to help you, even if you do not play a keyboard instrument
- **Always try to play, sing or tap the music you write.** This is a very important part of learning, and will help you 'hear' what you write in your head. It will help you in the exam when you have to work in silence

Learn on your own

- Use extra manuscript paper to practise transposition
- Use extra manuscript paper to practise writing melodies; in your exam you can choose whether you use the start that is given (though clef, time signature, instrument and tonality are prescribed)
- Composers of particular relevance to this grade are those writing in the Baroque period (approx. 1600–1750), eg **J S Bach**, **Corelli**, **Couperin**, **Handel**, **Marcello**, **Rameau**, **A and D Scarlatti**, **Telemann** and **Vivaldi**
- Play the music of the period and listen to recordings of the music mentioned in the Form section (see page 65)
- Read about the composers' lives
- Find out about the differences between modern instruments and those played in the Baroque period (today known as **period instruments**)
- Music of a period has a cultural context; it will help your understanding if you find out about the visual art, drama and architecture of the time; also about the social role of composers in that period

What comes next?

When you have finished this book try some sample papers. You will then be ready to ask your teacher to enter you for the Grade 6 Theory of Music exam.

To purchase past papers go to:
trinitycollege.com/qualifications/music/grade-exams/theory/past-papers

To purchase digital theory practice tests go to:
trinitycollege.com/qualifications/music/grade-exams/theory/digital-music-theory/practice-tests

To find out more about Trinity's Theory of Music exams please refer to:
trinitycollege.com/theory

Note values and rests

Demisemiquaver triplets

Sometimes composers want to divide a semiquaver into three equal parts. To do this they write **demisemiquaver triplets** – three demisemiquavers to be played in the time of two.

For example:

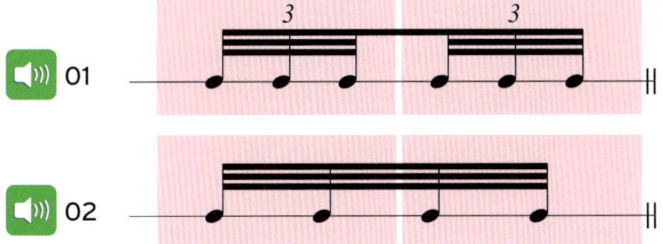

Sometimes, where two demisemiquaver triplets appear one after the other, they can be written like this (six in the time of four):

As with quaver and semiquaver triplets, sometimes composers want to use rests within demisemiquaver triplet groupings. You must bracket all demisemiquaver triplets where a rest or semiquaver is included in the triplet grouping.

1 Write 2-bar rhythms. Include demisemiquaver triplets.

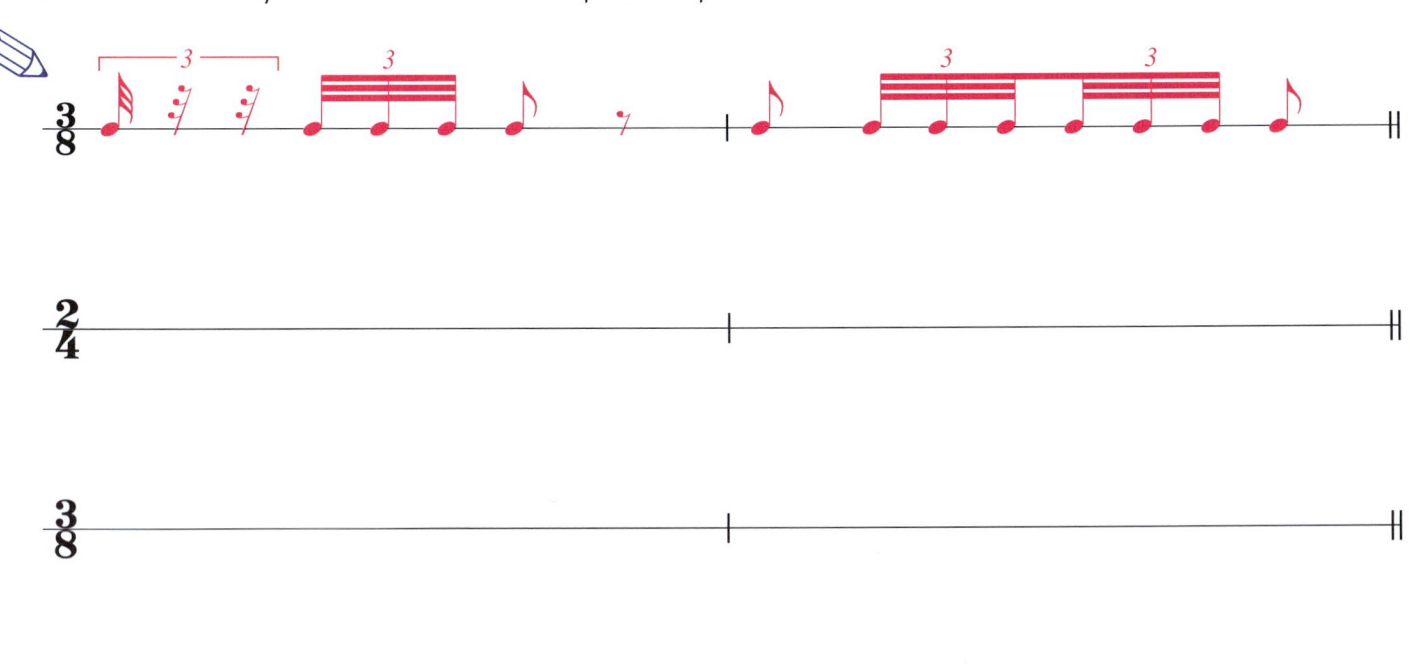

2 Add correct time signatures to the music.

Yandell

a

Dvořák

b

Haydn

c

Lizogub

d

Lizogub

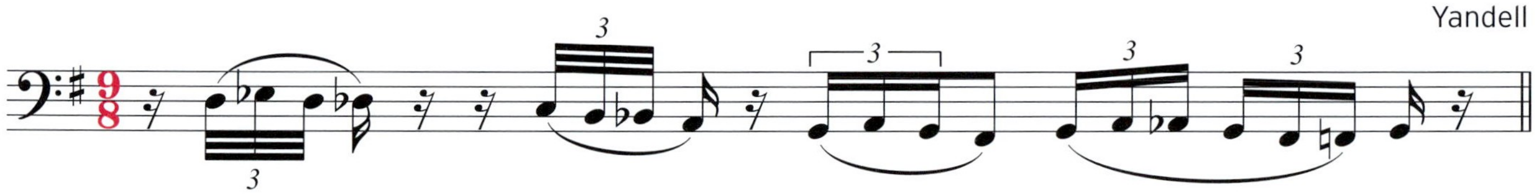

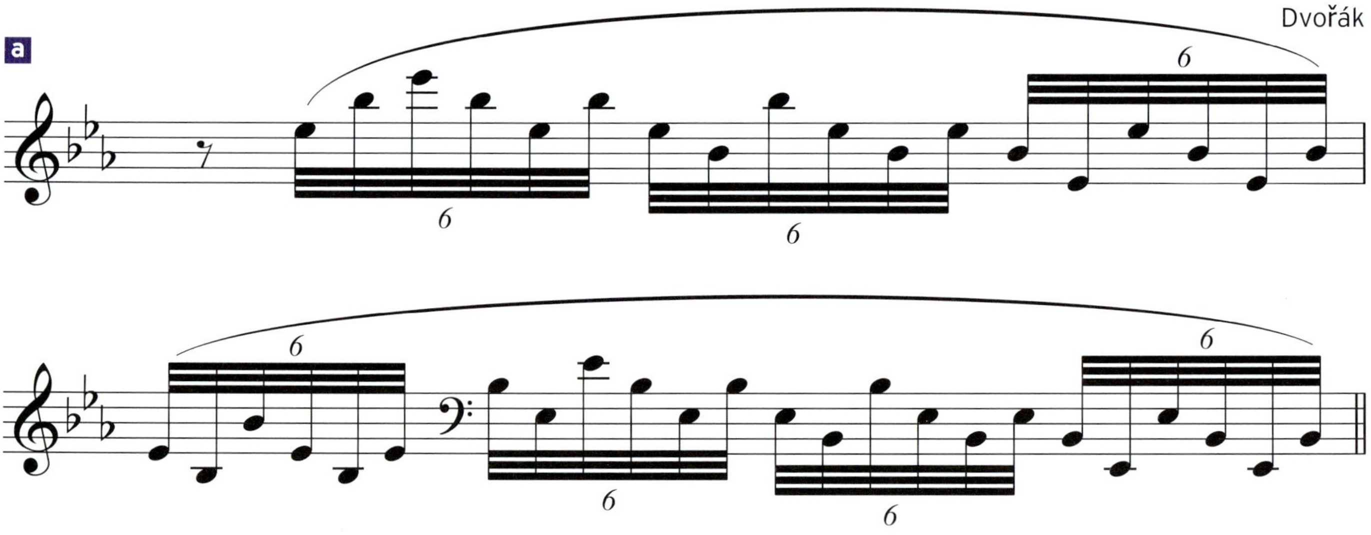

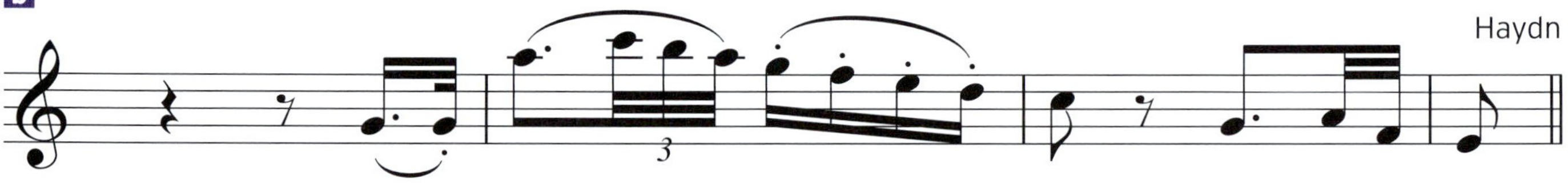

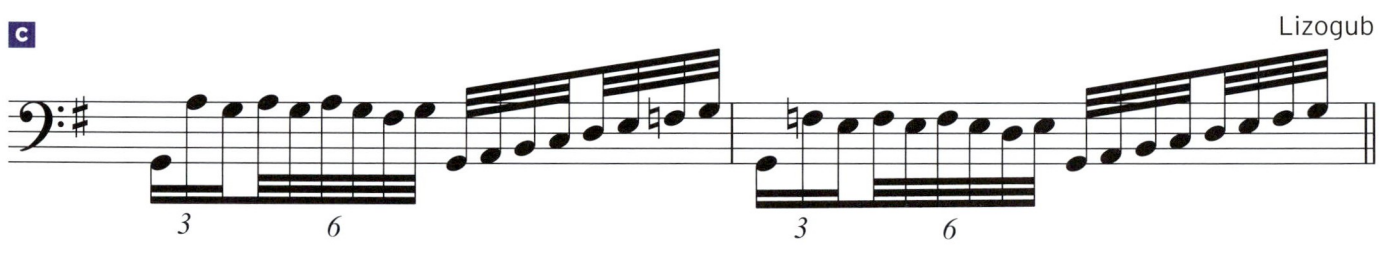

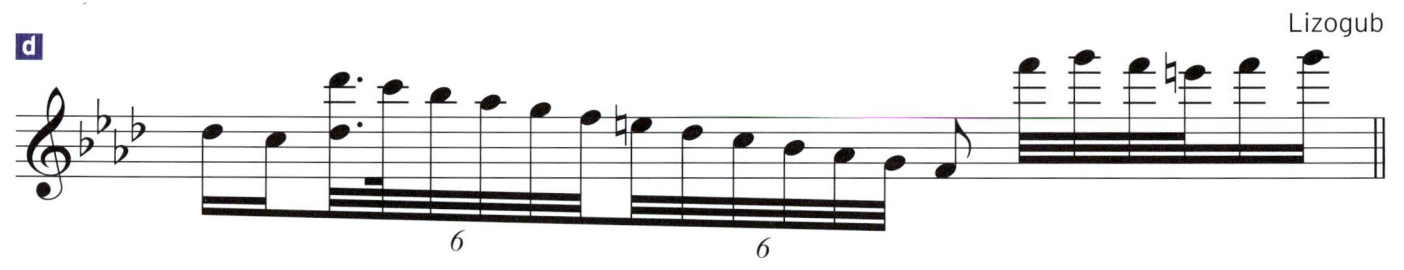

Double dotted notes and rests

As you know, a dot after a note means that half its value again is added to its length; if another dot is added, half the value of the first dot is also added, for example:

 + 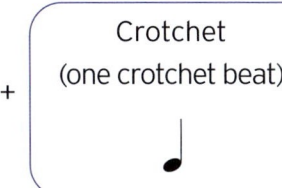 + 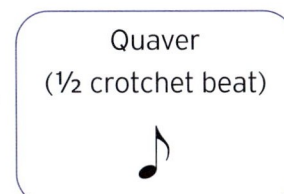 =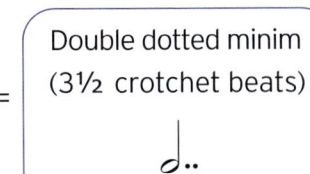

Rests can be double dotted too.

1 Write 2-bar rhythms. Include at least two double dotted notes and/or rests.

Duplets

Duplets are used most commonly by composers writing in compound time who want to divide the beat into two equal parts where the beat is usually divided into threes.

The rhythms below (shown in compound time then simple time) sound the same even though they are written differently:

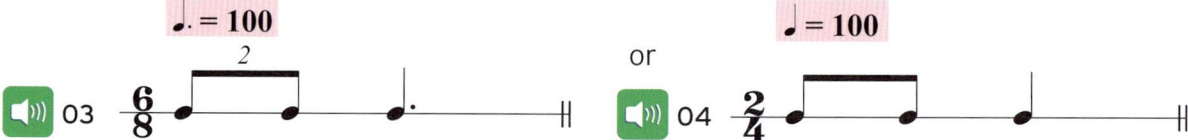

Sometimes composers writing in simple triple time want to divide the bar into two, rather than three. To do this they can either write:

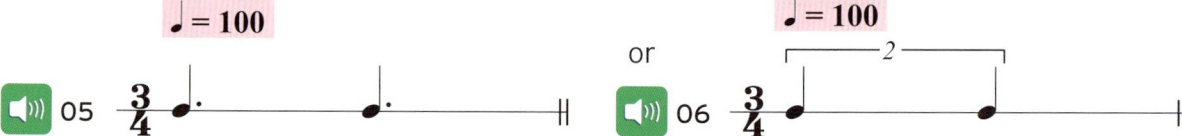

The rhythms shown above sound the same even though they are written differently. The duplet is often considered clearer for the player because the time signature is in simple time.

As with triplets, you must bracket all duplets where there is a rest or several different note values in the grouping; also where the number of beats in a bar would be unclear without one.

1 Write duplets to agree with each time signature.

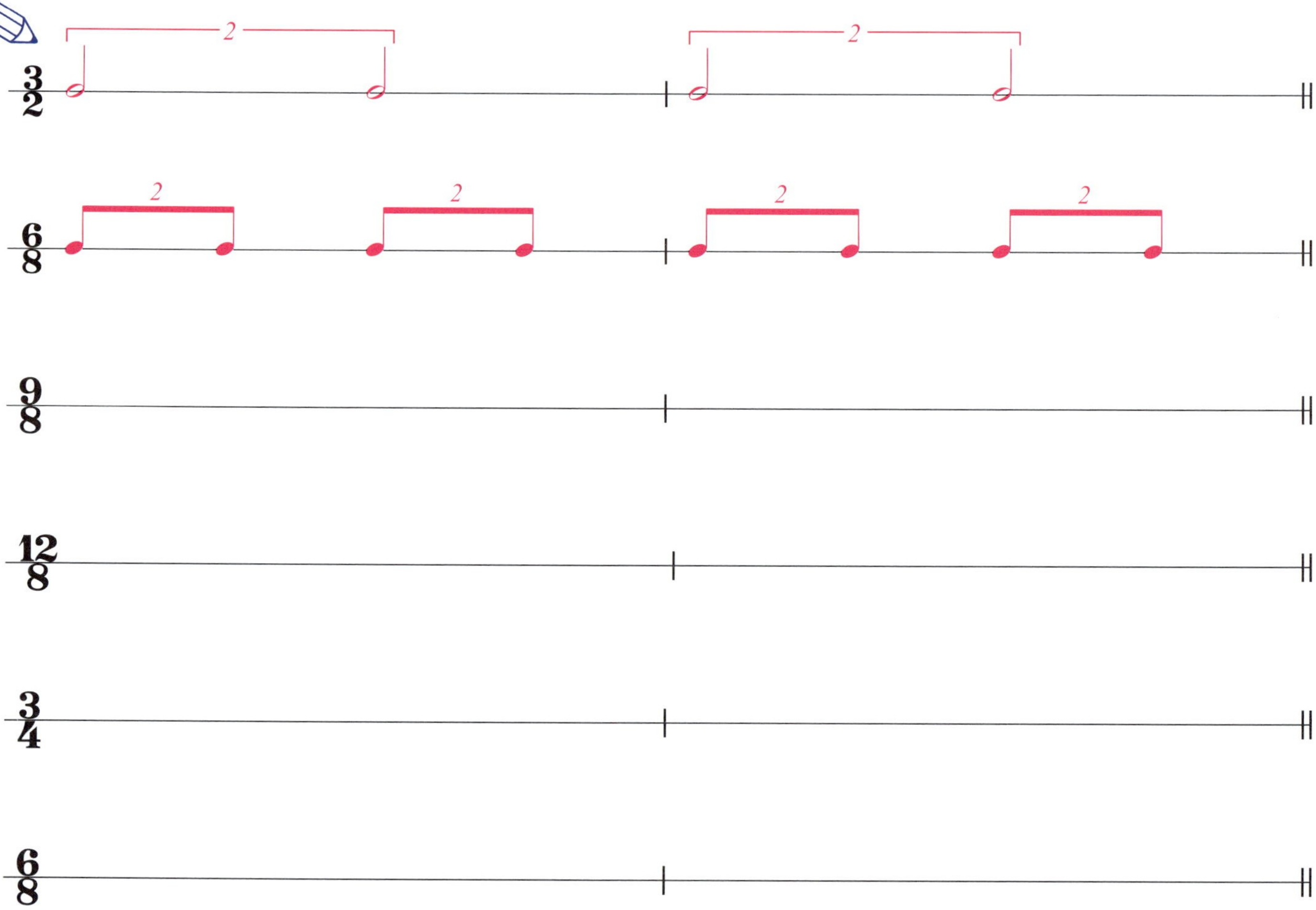

2 Add correct time signatures to the music.

a
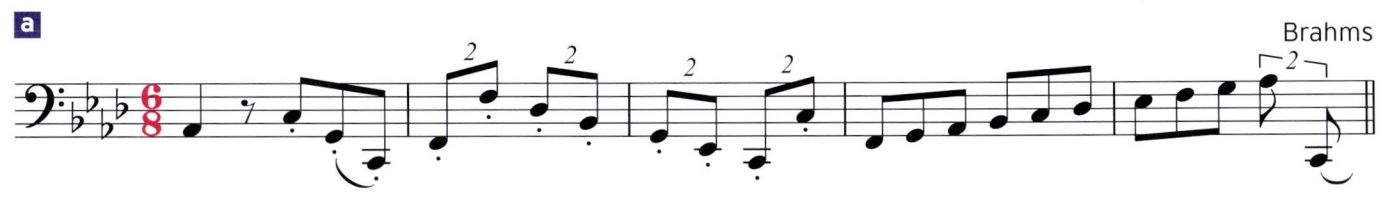
Brahms

b

Fauré

c
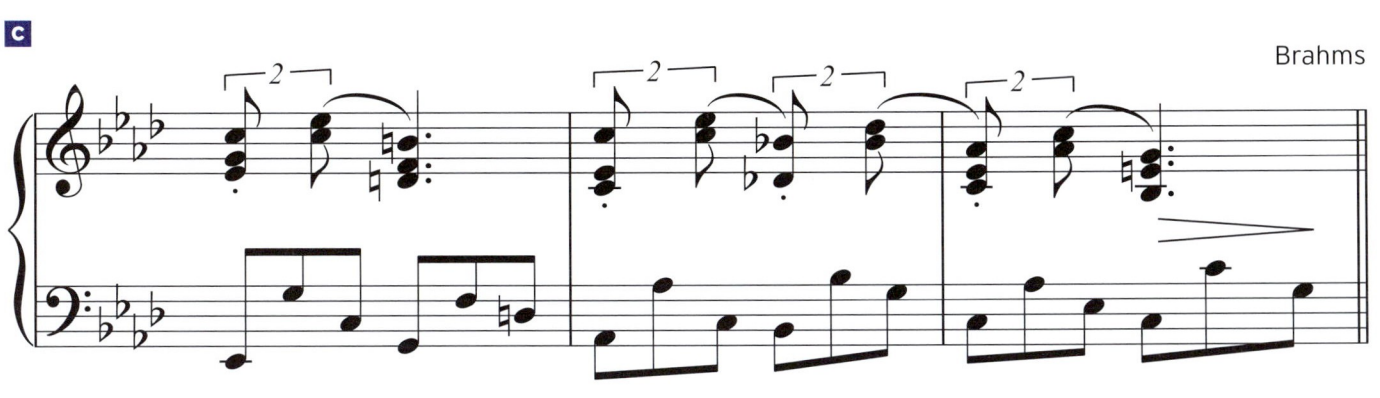
Brahms

d

Janáček

e
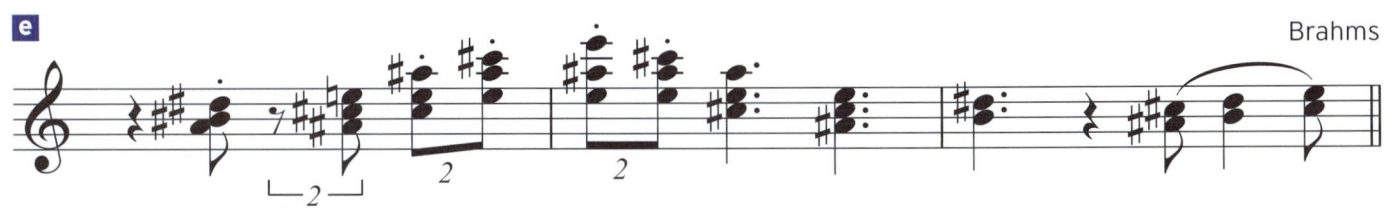
Brahms

3 Add appropriate duplets in the places marked by an asterisk (*) to complete the arpeggios.

4 Write 2-bar rhythms using the note values and rests you know. Include duplets.

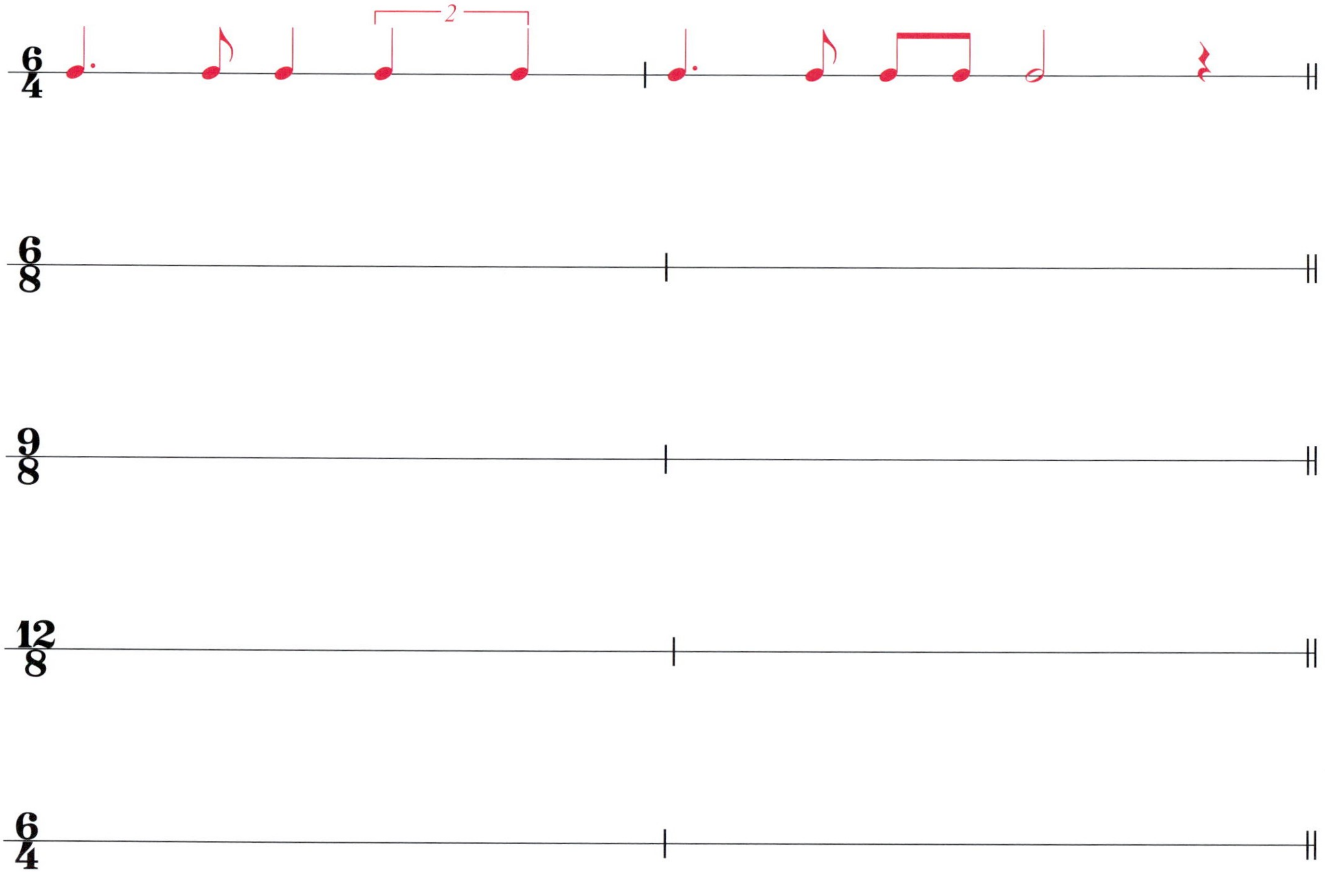

Hemiola

Hemiola is a Greek word that describes the ratio of 3:2.

A hemiola occurs when a composer switches the main beat of the bar for one (or more) bars, often on the approach to a cadence. This is done without changing the time signature and has the effect of altering the stress of the beats in the bar from two to three beats. The harmonic rhythm often changes too. Hemiolas are quite common in the French **courante**, a dance often included in the Baroque suite (see page 68).

Here is an example; the coloured boxes help you see the main beats:

F Couperin

07 **Courante**

Play or listen to as many courantes as you can to get the feel of hemiolas.
Note The ornaments in this section have been left out for clarity.
NB Beaming often shows where hemiolas are in use.

Did you know?

Many composers, not only Baroque composers, use hemiolas in their music, though in a less formalised way. For example:

Mozart

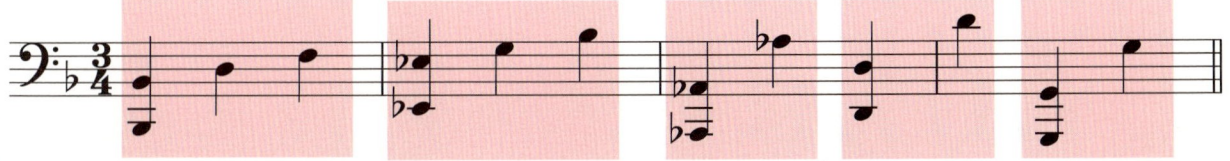

Playlist: Hemiola

- Bernstein & Sondheim: America (from West Side Story) (0:52 onwards frequently switches from 3, 3 to 2, 2, 2)
- Beatles: Here Comes the Sun (0:23)

1 Bracket (⌐——¬) the main beats to show where they change to create a hemiola effect. The first two beats have been done for you.

a

🔊 08

F Couperin

b

🔊 09

F Couperin

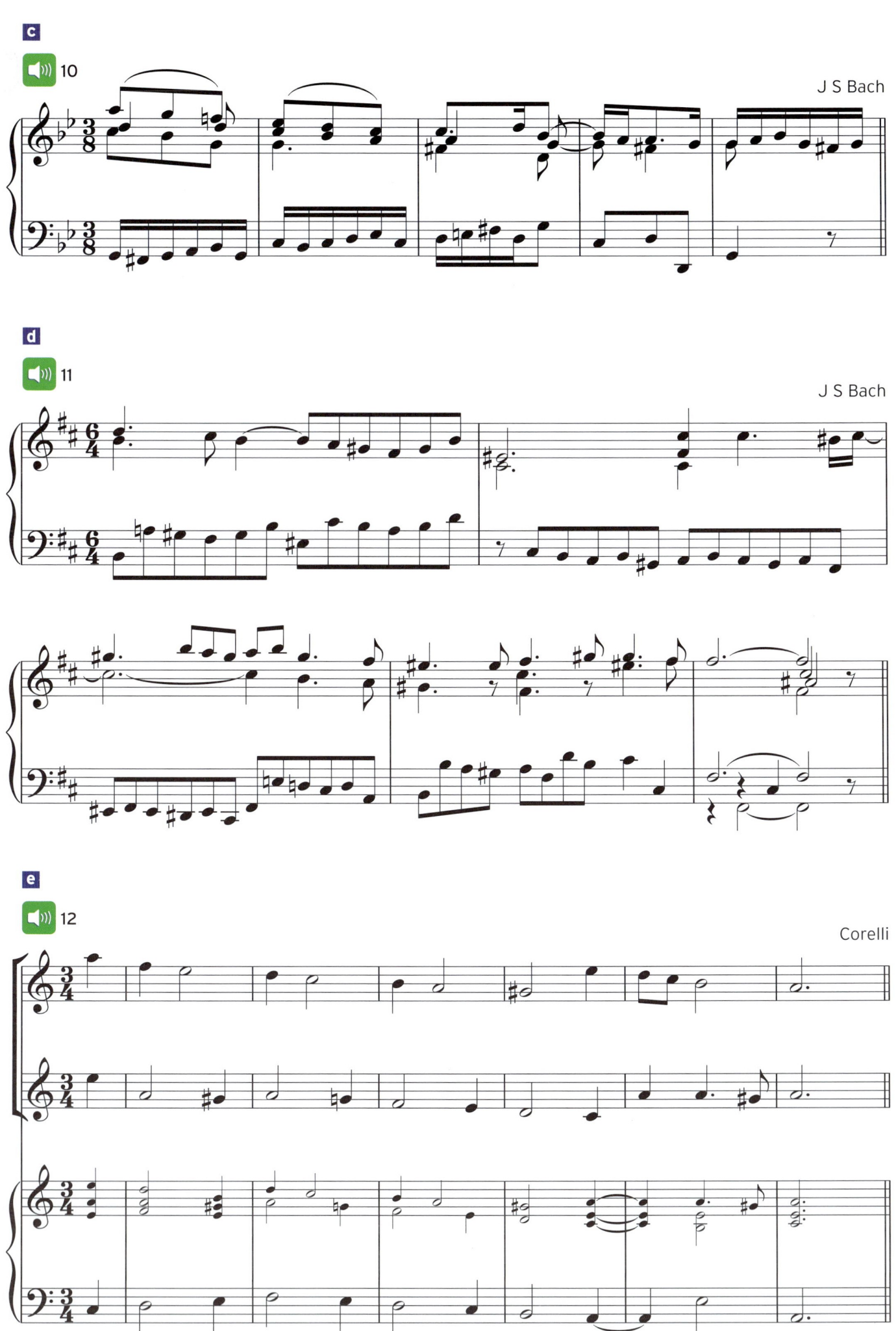

Swung quavers

In jazz you will often see the following: ♫ = ♩♪ (triplet)

This instruction is used where composers write quavers but want the musician to play ♩♪ (triplet)

 **Playlist: Swing**

- Bob Russell & Duke Ellington: Don't Get Around Much Anymore
- Jimmy Van Heusen & Sammy Cahn: Ain't That A Kick In The Head
- Benny Goodman: Sing, Sing Sing

1 Write this music as a player should perform it.

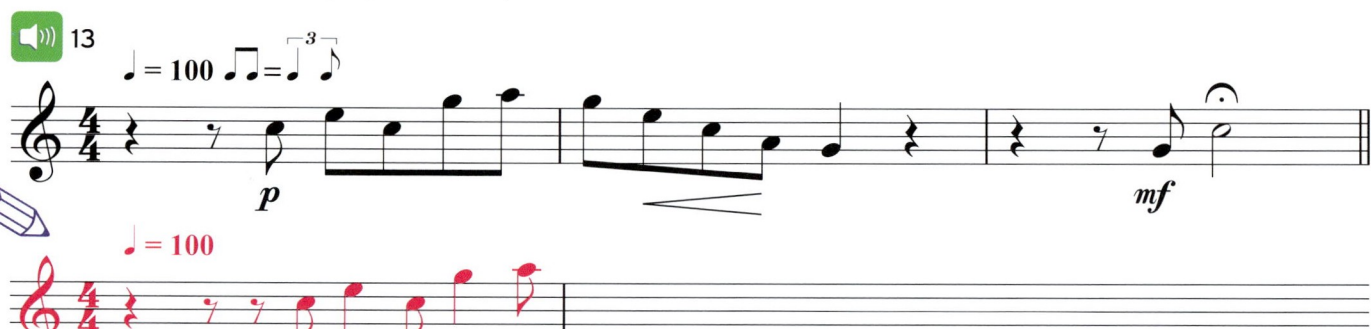

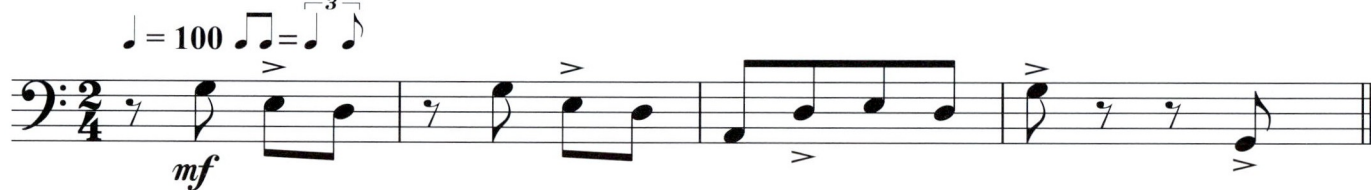

NB The following rhythms sound the same even though they are written differently:

 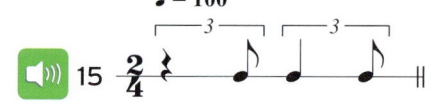 

Scales and melody writing

Pentatonic major scales

As you will remember from Grade 5, the pentatonic major scale is made up of five notes and is played like a major scale without the 4th and 7th degrees.

D pentatonic major scale

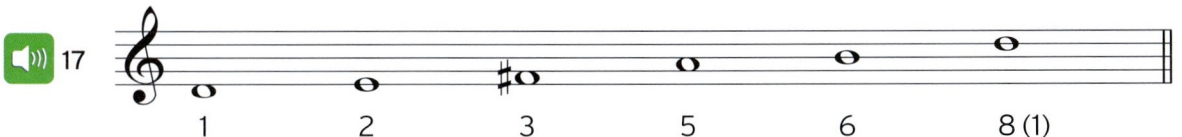

For Grade 6 you need to know C, D, F and G pentatonic major scales.

Playlist: Major Pentatonic Melodies

- Trad: Swing Low, Sweet Chariot
- Jack Johnson: Better Together
- The Temptations: My Girl
- Pentatonix: Amazing Grace (My Chains Are Gone)
- James Taylor: Auld Lang Syne
- Katy Perry: Roar

1 Write out the following one-octave scales in a rhythm to fit the given time signature. Use rests between some degrees of the scale. Do not use key signatures but write in the necessary accidentals.

D pentatonic major scale ascending then descending

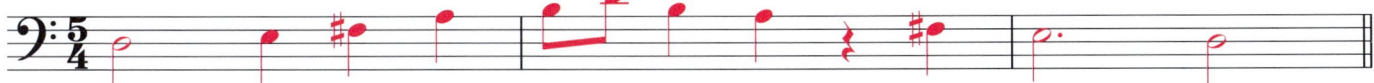

G pentatonic major scale descending then ascending

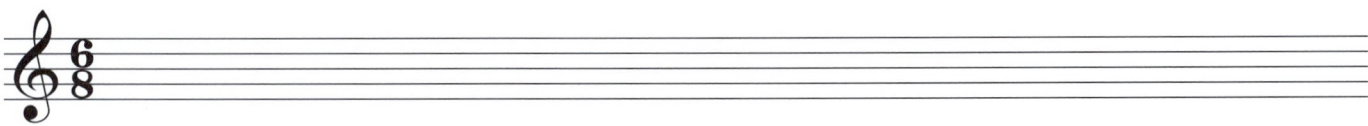

F pentatonic major scale ascending then descending

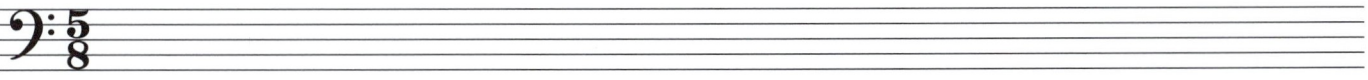

D pentatonic major scale descending then ascending

C pentatonic major scale descending then ascending

> ### Remember
> A note lasting a full bar in 4/2 is called a breve: ‖o‖
> Unusually, the semibreve rest (used in every other time signature as a whole bar of silence) is not used in 4/2; a breve rest is used instead, filling up the whole space between the two lines of the stave:

> ### Handy tip!
> When writing a melody:
> - balance the shape of phrases and cadence points
> - consider using rests, sequences and repetition
> - consider where the high-point (or climax) of your melody should be
> - always play or sing your melody to check that it sounds as you think it does in your head.

> ### Handy tip!
> When writing for a specific instrument or voice:
> - write well within its range (use the highest and lowest notes sparingly for the climax of a piece or for a special effect)
> - be aware that it is usually difficult for players to play the highest and lowest notes of their instruments
> - use techniques that work well on the instrument (eg pizz. etc (bowed string instruments) – see page 72)
> - think of practicalities; singers and wind players must have time to breathe between phrases; string players need time to change from pizz. to arco etc
> - find out what sounds good on a particular instrument (this will help you write **idiomatic music** for it – that is music that plays to the instrument's strengths, eg fast scales and arpeggios are generally more easily playable on treble instruments, brass music often uses a lot of arpeggio features etc.)
> - add dynamics and articulation markings to make your music more interesting
> - for a reminder of instrument ranges see page 87.

2 Write 8-bar melodies using notes from pentatonic major scales. Do not use key signatures but write in the necessary accidentals. Write at written (rather than sounding) pitch for transposing instruments.

For cello using F pentatonic major

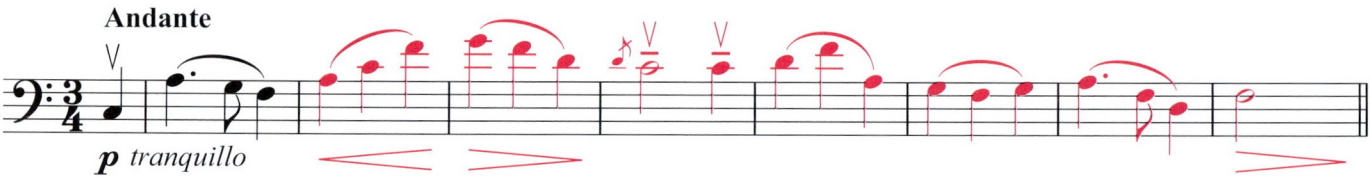

a For alto saxophone in E♭ using C pentatonic major

mf espressivo

b For trumpet in B♭ using F pentatonic major

f pesante

c For clarinet in B♭ using D pentatonic major

mp legato

Pentatonic minor scales

A **pentatonic minor scale** is made up of five notes and is played like a natural minor scale without the 2nd and 6th degrees.

For Grade 6 you need to know the pentatonic minor scales starting on **A**, **B**, **D** and **E**.

Here is **A pentatonic minor scale**:

 18

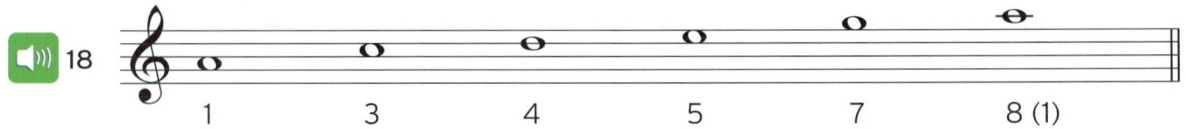

1   3   4   5   7   8 (1)

NB As with C major and A natural minor scales, the notes of the C pentatonic major and A pentatonic minor scales are exactly the same but written in a different order; the first degree of the scale is A not C, which gives a different focus to the music.

Playlist: Minor Pentatonic Melodies

- Wild Cherry: Play That Funky Music
- Joan Jett & the Blackhearts: I Love Rock 'N Roll
- Stevie Wonder: Superstition
- Queen: We Will Rock You
- Avicii: Hey Brother

1 Write out the following one-octave scales in a rhythm to fit the given time signature. Use rests between some degrees of the scale. Do not use key signatures but write in the necessary accidentals.

B pentatonic minor scale ascending then descending

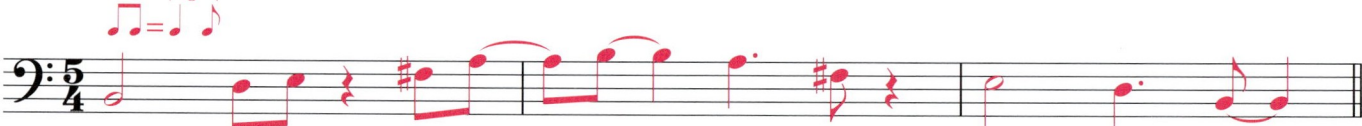

A pentatonic minor scale descending then ascending

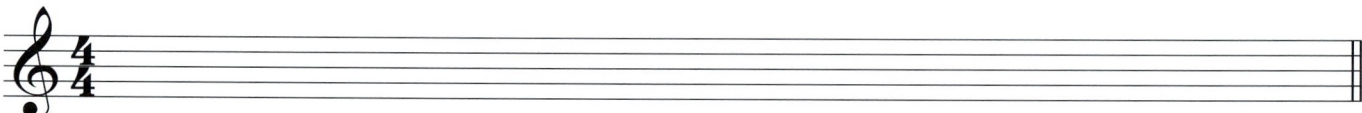

D pentatonic minor scale ascending then descending

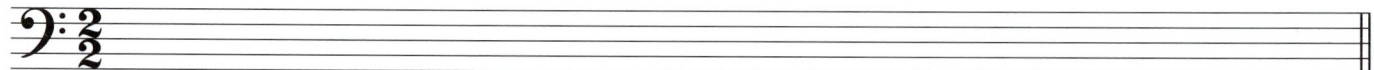

E pentatonic minor scale descending then ascending

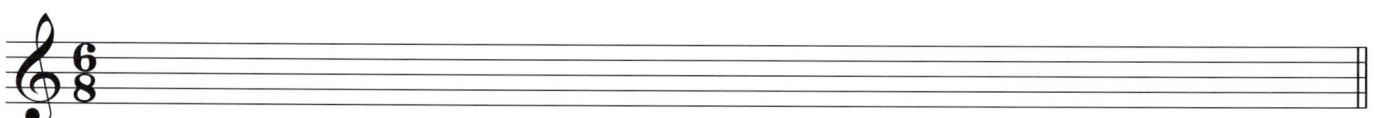

B pentatonic minor scale ascending then descending

2 Write 8-bar melodies using notes from pentatonic minor scales. Do not use key signatures but write in the necessary accidentals. Write at written (rather than sounding) pitch for transposing instruments.

For trumpet in B♭ using D pentatonic minor

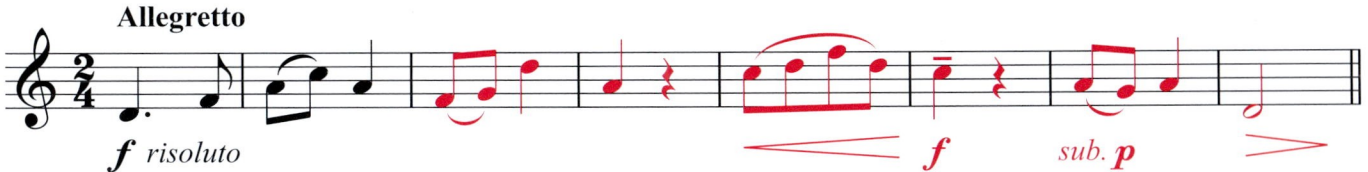

a For descant recorder using B pentatonic minor

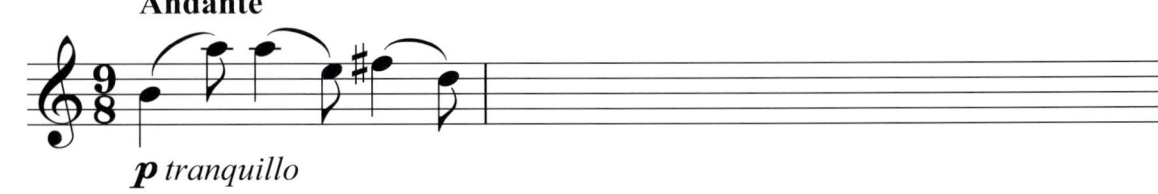

b For bassoon using E pentatonic minor

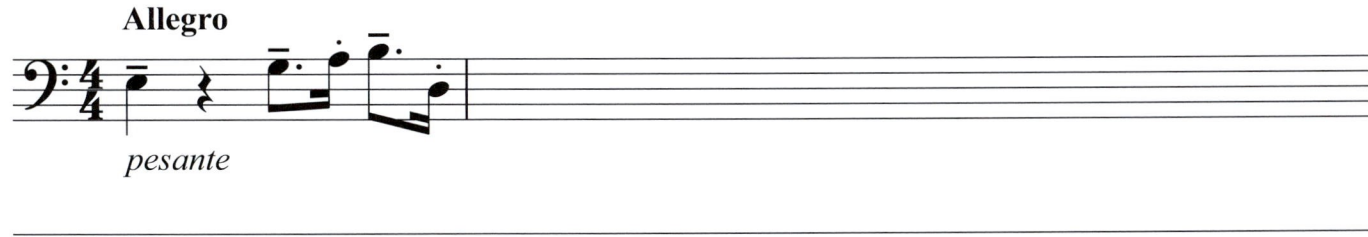

c For violin using D pentatonic minor

Handy tip!
In your exam you may choose whether or not you use the start that is given (though clef, time signature, instrument and tonality are prescribed).

Use extra manuscript paper to practise writing melodies.

Blues scales

The **blues scale** is the same as the pentatonic minor scale but with an extra **blue note** shown in the coloured box. For Grade 6 you need to know the blues scales starting on **A**, **B**, **D** and **E**.

Here is the **A** blues scale:

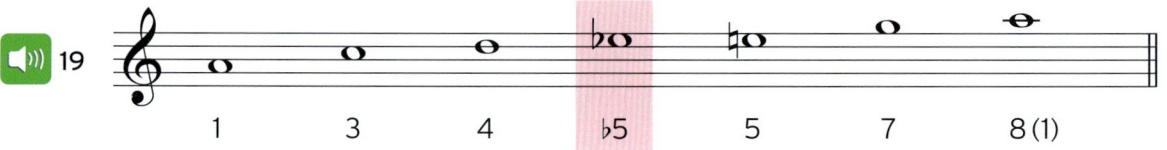

Playlist: Blues Scale Melodies

- B.B. King; Tracy Chapman: The Thrill Is Gone
- Nina Simone: Feeling Good
- Christina Aguilera: Walk Away

1 Write out the following one-octave scales in a rhythm to fit the given time signature. Use rests between some degrees of the scale. Do not use key signatures but write in the necessary accidentals.

A blues scale ascending then descending

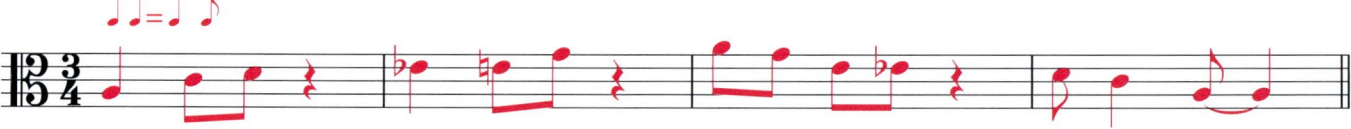

D blues scale descending then ascending

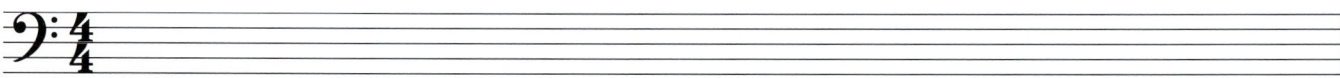

B blues scale ascending then descending

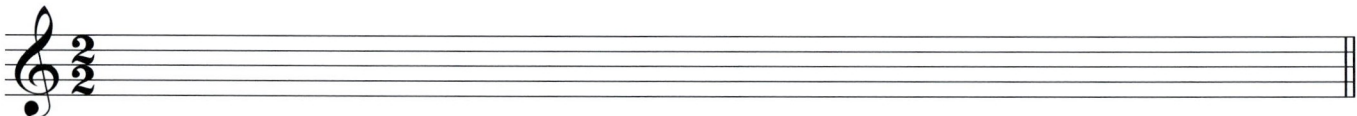

A blues scale descending then ascending

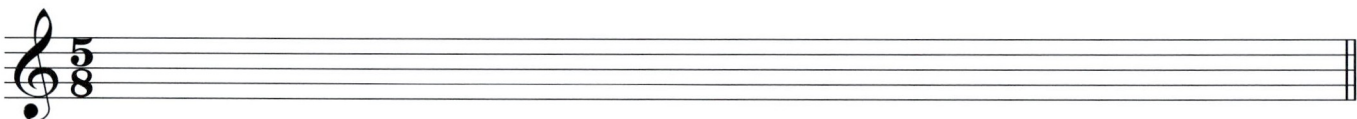

E blues scale descending then ascending

2 Write 8-bar melodies using notes from blues scales. Do not use key signatures but write in the necessary accidentals. Write at written (rather than sounding) pitch for transposing instruments.

Handy tip!
Blues scales may focus in different places (for example, in E blues scale the focus may be on **E** or **G**. The example given focuses on **G**.)

For flute using E blues scale, focusing on G

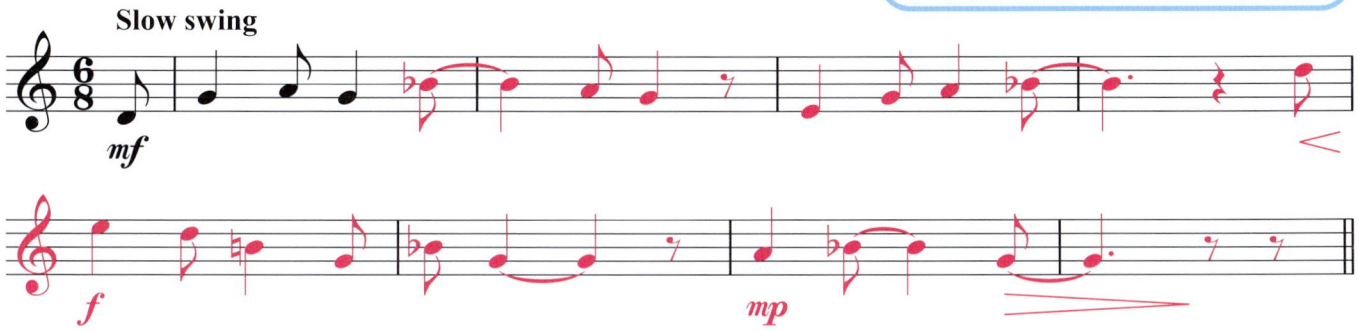

a For cello using B blues scale, focusing on B

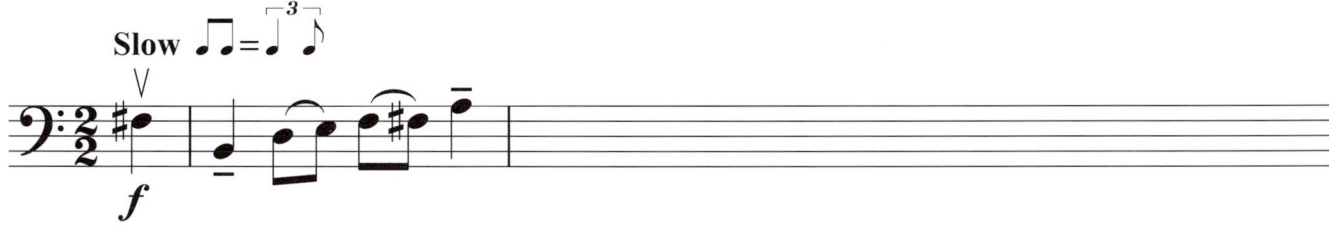

b For trumpet in B♭ using A blues scale, focusing on C

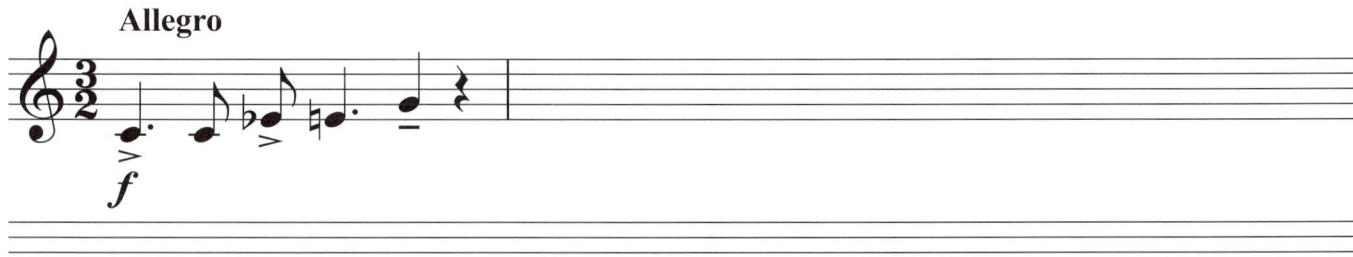

c For treble recorder using D blues scale, focusing on D

Modes

You have now composed melodies using scales other than major and minor scales. The major/minor system developed from the modal system – where there are many tone-semitone patterns on which to base melody and harmony. **Modes** are still used in many types of music today.

The easiest way to understand how some of the many modes work is to play every white note on a keyboard starting on different notes (**A-A**, or **F-F** etc). Notice that the tone-semitone pattern changes each time you start a scale on a different note, for example:

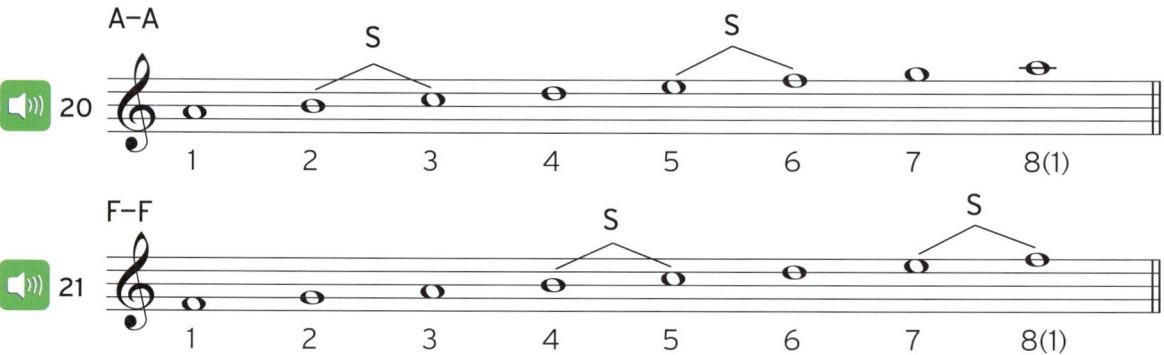

You will recognise **A-A** as the natural minor scale. You now need to know that this can also be called the **Aeolian mode**. Here it is transposed to start on **F** (F natural minor). Notice that accidentals are necessary to keep the tone-semitone pattern correct for the Aeolian mode.

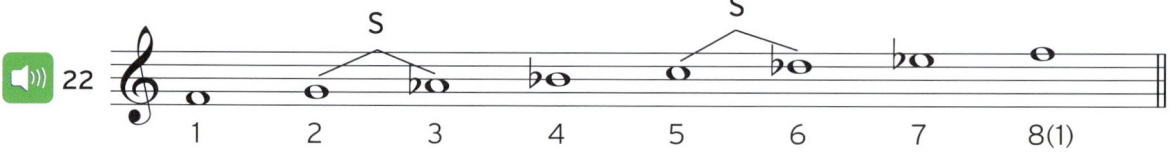

1 Write out the Aeolian mode starting on these notes. Mark the semitones.

G-G

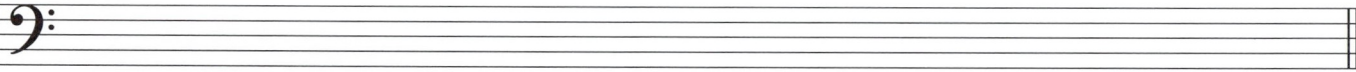

D-D

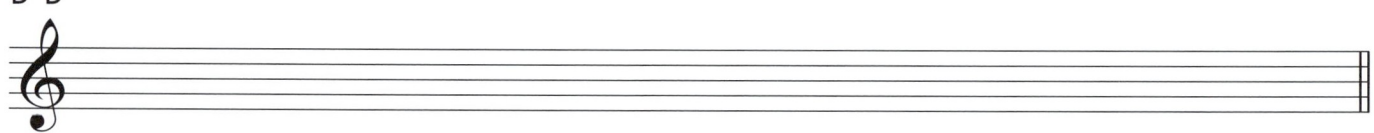

E-E

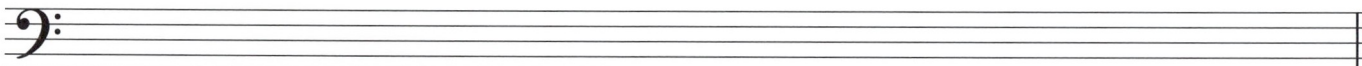

Playlist: Aeolian Mode

- Ozzy Osbourne: Crazy Train
- Black Sabbath: Paranoid
- Jimi Hendrix: All Along the Watchtower
- R.E.M.: Losing My Religion
- Nirvana: Smells Like Teen Spirit
- Avicii: Hey Brother
- Fleetwood Mac: The Chain
- Adele: Hello

Working out the key or mode of a piece

Many melodies, especially folk ballads (see page 71), are written using the Aeolian mode and for Grade 6 you need to be able to recognise and write them.

Here is an example to show how to work out whether music is written using the Aeolian mode:

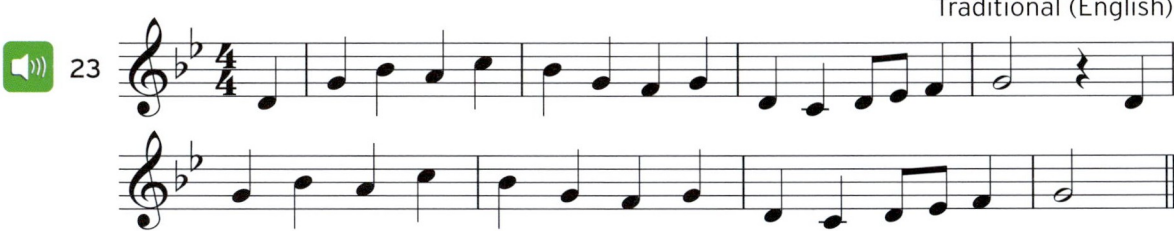

- Are there flats or sharps in the key signature and if so, how many? Yes, two flats, so the key could be B flat major or G minor, or the music could be written using Aeolian mode starting on G (G natural minor)
- Are there any accidentals in the music that could be the raised 6th or 7th degrees in the relative minor? No
- Are there reasons to think that the key is B flat major? No, the phrases are focused around G and its dominant, D

Answer: This melody is written using Aeolian mode starting on G

1 Use the questions above to work out the key or mode.

Key or mode: _____

Traditional (English)

Key or mode: _____

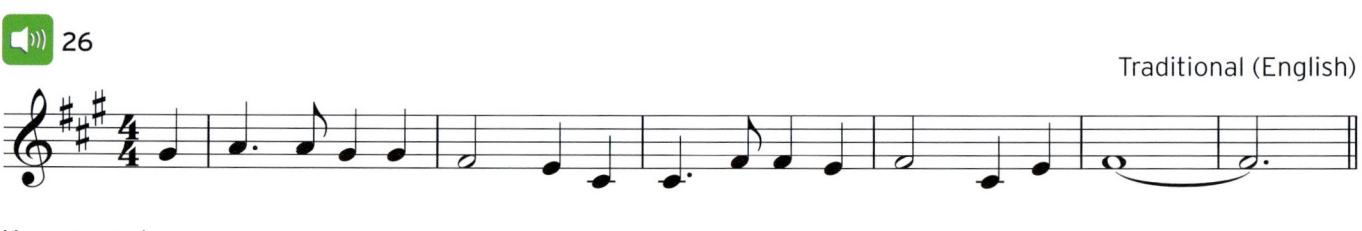

Traditional (English)

Key or mode: _____

2 Write 8-bar melodies using notes from the Aeolian mode. Use key signatures. Write at written pitch (rather than sounding) for transposing instruments.

For violin using Aeolian mode starting on F#

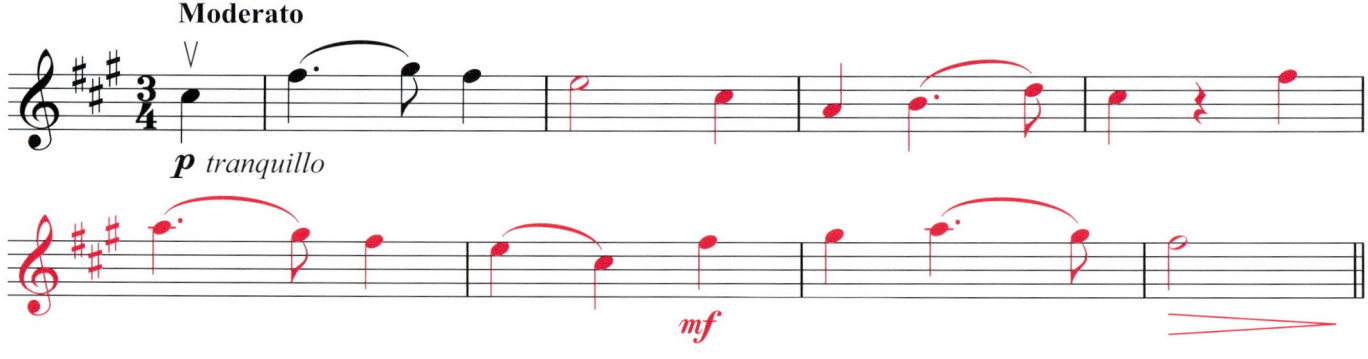

a For clarinet in A using Aeolian mode starting on B

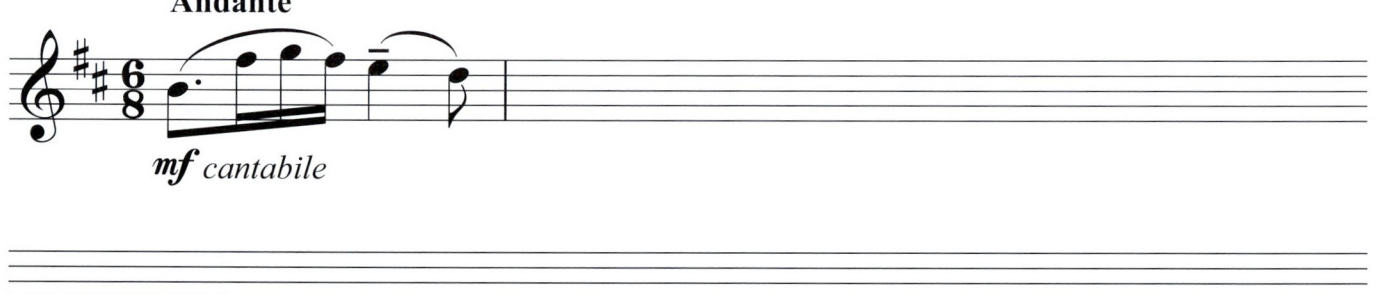

b For viola using Aeolian mode starting on C

c For guitar using Aeolian mode starting on E

The circle of 5ths

Here is the circle of 5ths showing all the major and minor keys. You need to know these for Grade 6.

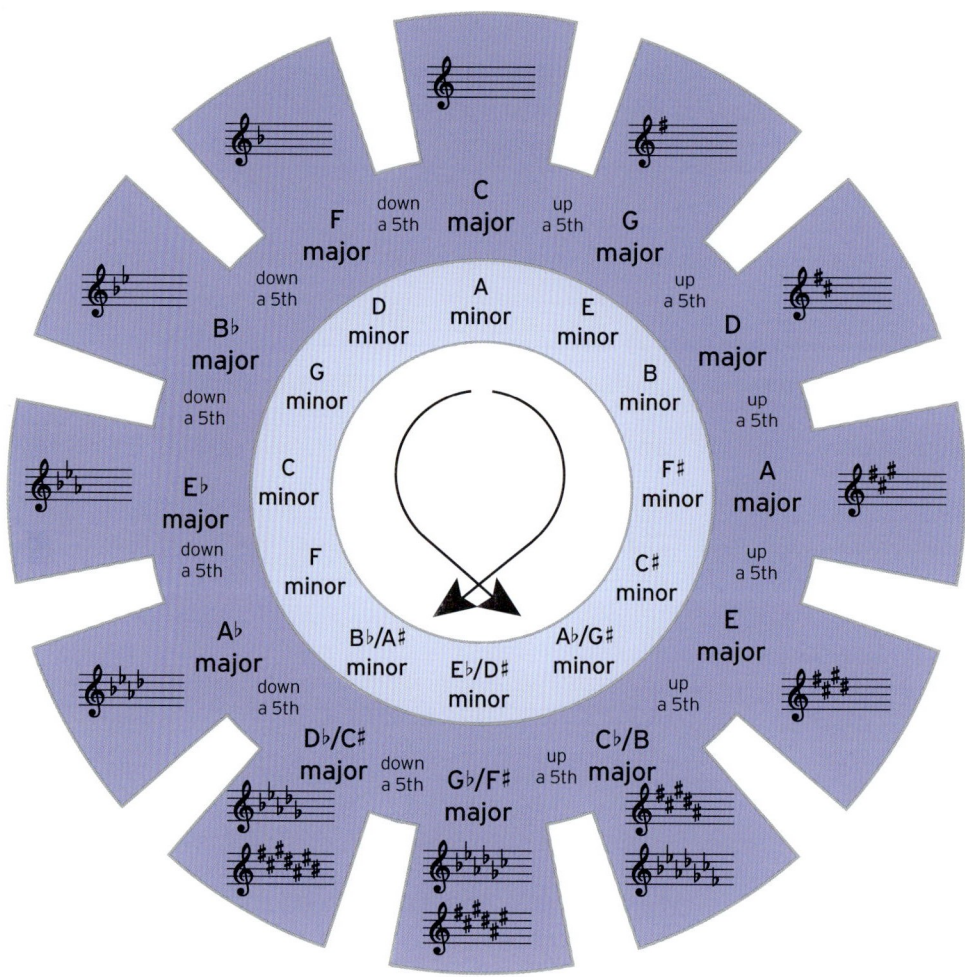

NB The new keys for this grade are enharmonically equivalent to other keys, ie a composer can choose whether to write in G flat major or F sharp major. Some of these keys are not used often but you should know them and be able to use them.

Using the circle of 5ths above, answer these questions:

1. Which major key has six flats in its key signature? _____
2. Which minor key has seven sharps in its key signaure? _____
3. Which major key is enharmonically equivalent to B major? _____
4. Which minor key is enharmonically equivalent to E flat minor? _____
5. Which major key is enharmonically equivalent to D flat major? _____
6. Which key is the relative major of E flat minor? _____
7. Which key is the relative minor of D flat major? _____
8. Which key is the relative major of A sharp minor? _____
9. Which key is the relative minor of C flat major? _____

More about the new key signatures for Grade 6

 The new keys for Grade 6 are F sharp, C sharp, G flat and C flat majors (and their relative minors D sharp, A sharp, E flat and A flat minors).

They work like the others you have learned; the key signatures are there to make sure that the tone-semitone pattern is the same for each key.

1 Write the key signature and the tonic triad in root position for each of the following keys.

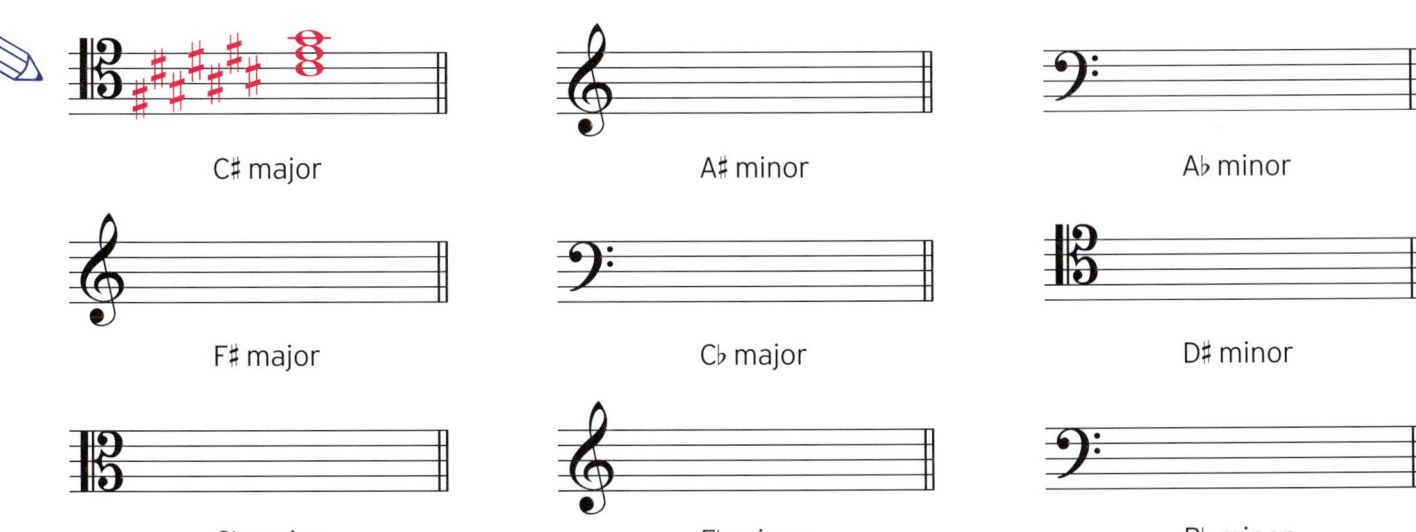

2 Write out the following one-octave scales in a rhythm to fit the given time signature. Use rests between some degrees of the scale. Use key signatures.

G♭ major descending then ascending

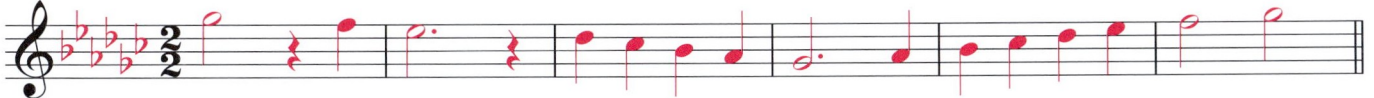

A♭ harmonic minor ascending then descending

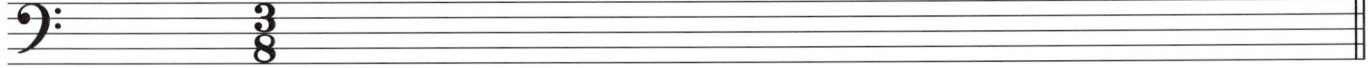

C♯ major descending then ascending

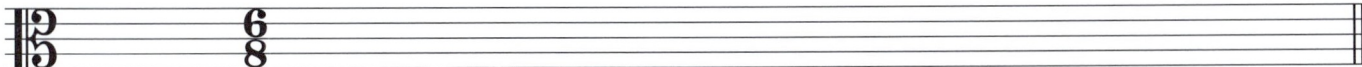

D♯ melodic minor descending then ascending

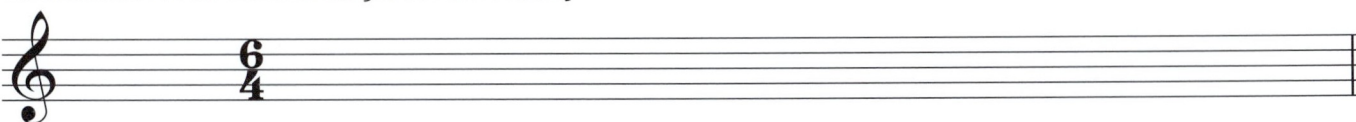

3 Write out the following one-octave scales in a rhythm to fit the given time signature. Use rests between some degrees of the scale. Do not use key signatures but write in the necessary accidentals.

F♯ major ascending then descending

C♭ major descending then ascending

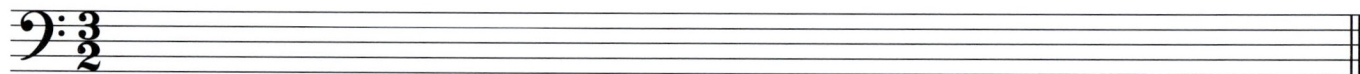

B♭ natural minor ascending then descending

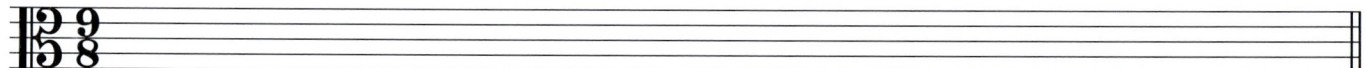

G♯ harmonic minor ascending then descending

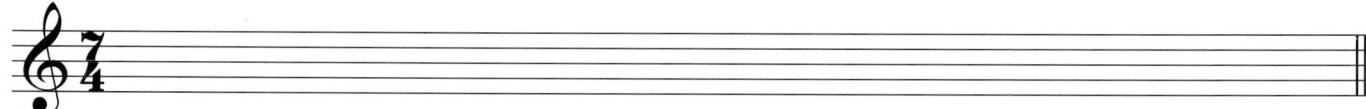

4 Write 8-bar melodies in major keys. Write at written (rather than sounding) pitch for transposing instruments.

a For oboe using F♯ major

b For flute using B major

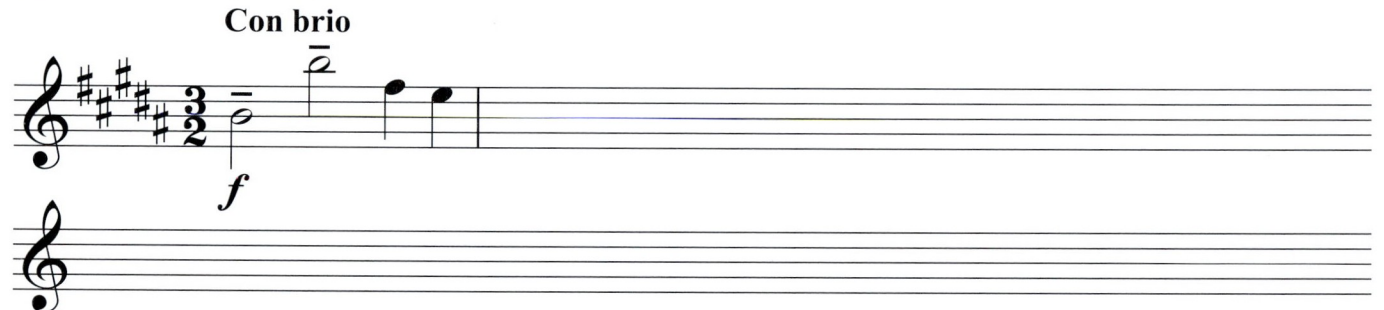

c For double bass using E major

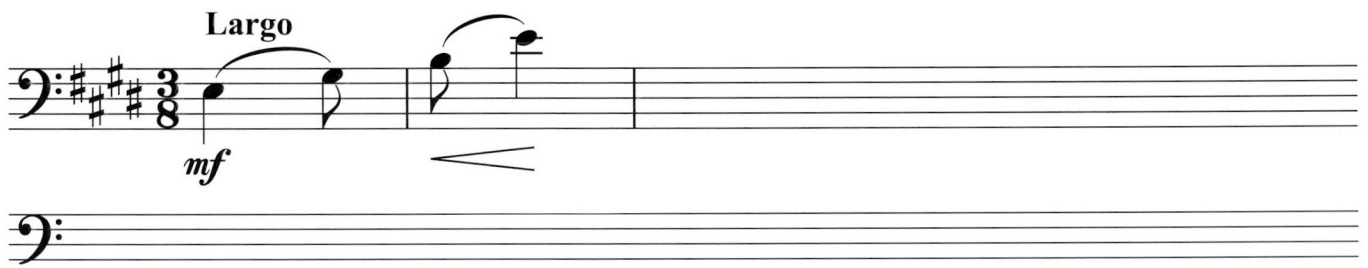

5 Write 8-bar melodies in minor keys. Write at written (rather than sounding) pitch for transposing instruments.

For cello using C♯ minor

For French horn in F using G minor

For bassoon using F minor

6 Circle the pairs of keys that are enharmonically equivalent.

| D sharp minor | C sharp minor | C sharp major | C flat major |
| E flat minor | D flat minor | D flat major | B major |

| C sharp minor | G flat major | A flat major | E flat minor |
| B minor | F sharp major | B flat major | D minor |

Arpeggios

1 Write the key signature for each key shown. Then write its one-octave arpeggio in a rhythm to fit the given time signature.

C♭ major descending then ascending

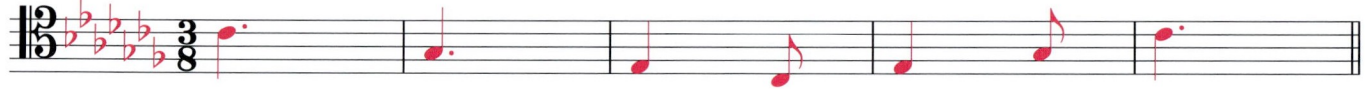

D♯ minor ascending then descending

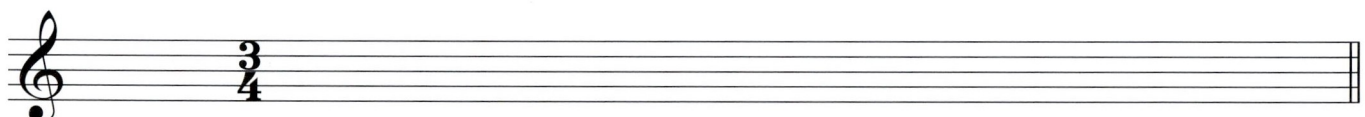

A♯ minor descending then ascending

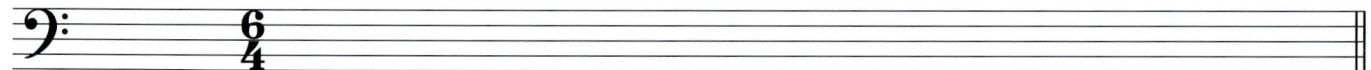

B♭ major ascending then descending

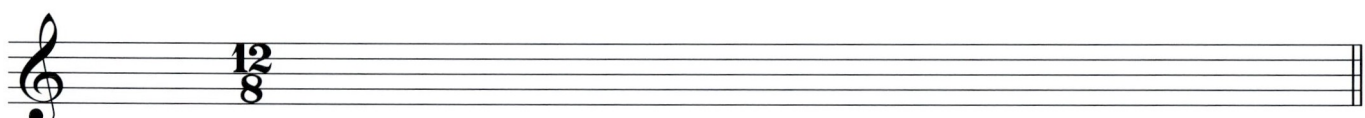

B minor ascending then descending

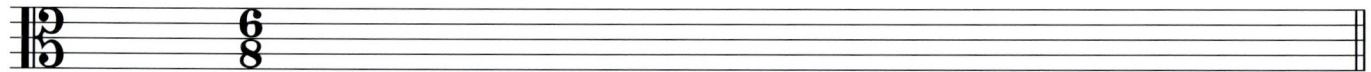

F♯ major descending then ascending

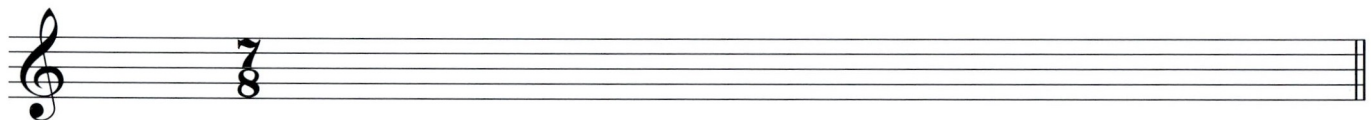

G♭ major descending then ascending

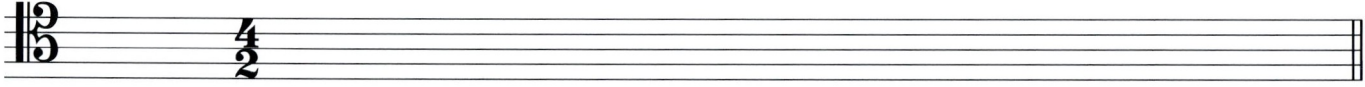

Transposing melodies

For Grade 6 you need to know how to transpose a melody for any transposing instrument for the grade. See page 87 for the instruments, ranges and which transposing intervals you need to memorise. Where the transposing interval is large you may need to write the music in another clef.

Remember
Use a key signature and add accidentals where necessary to keep the intervals the required distance apart.

1 Transpose this melody up a minor 3rd so that a clarinet in A will be able to play it at the same pitch as the following notes.

2 Transpose this melody so that a tenor saxophone in B flat will be able to play it at the same pitch as the following notes.

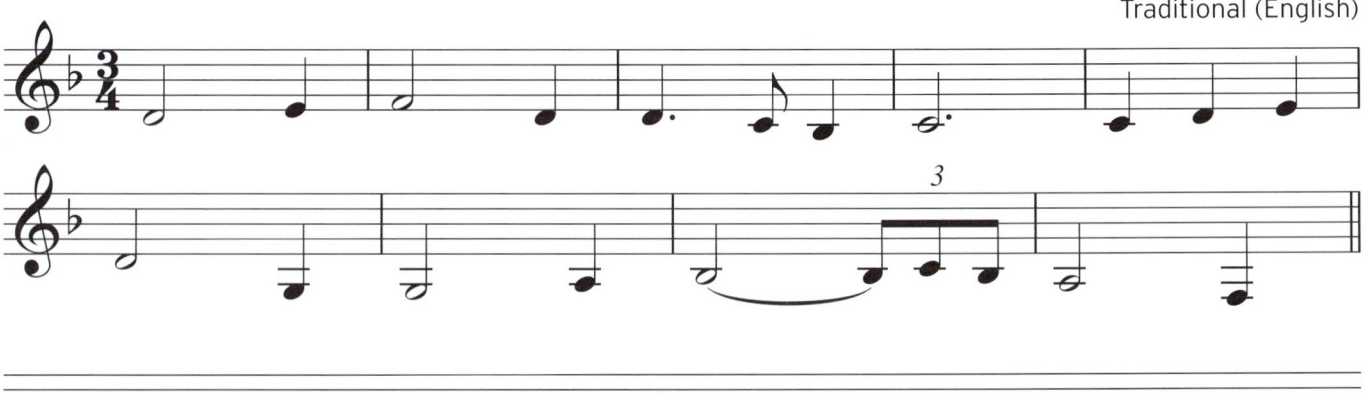

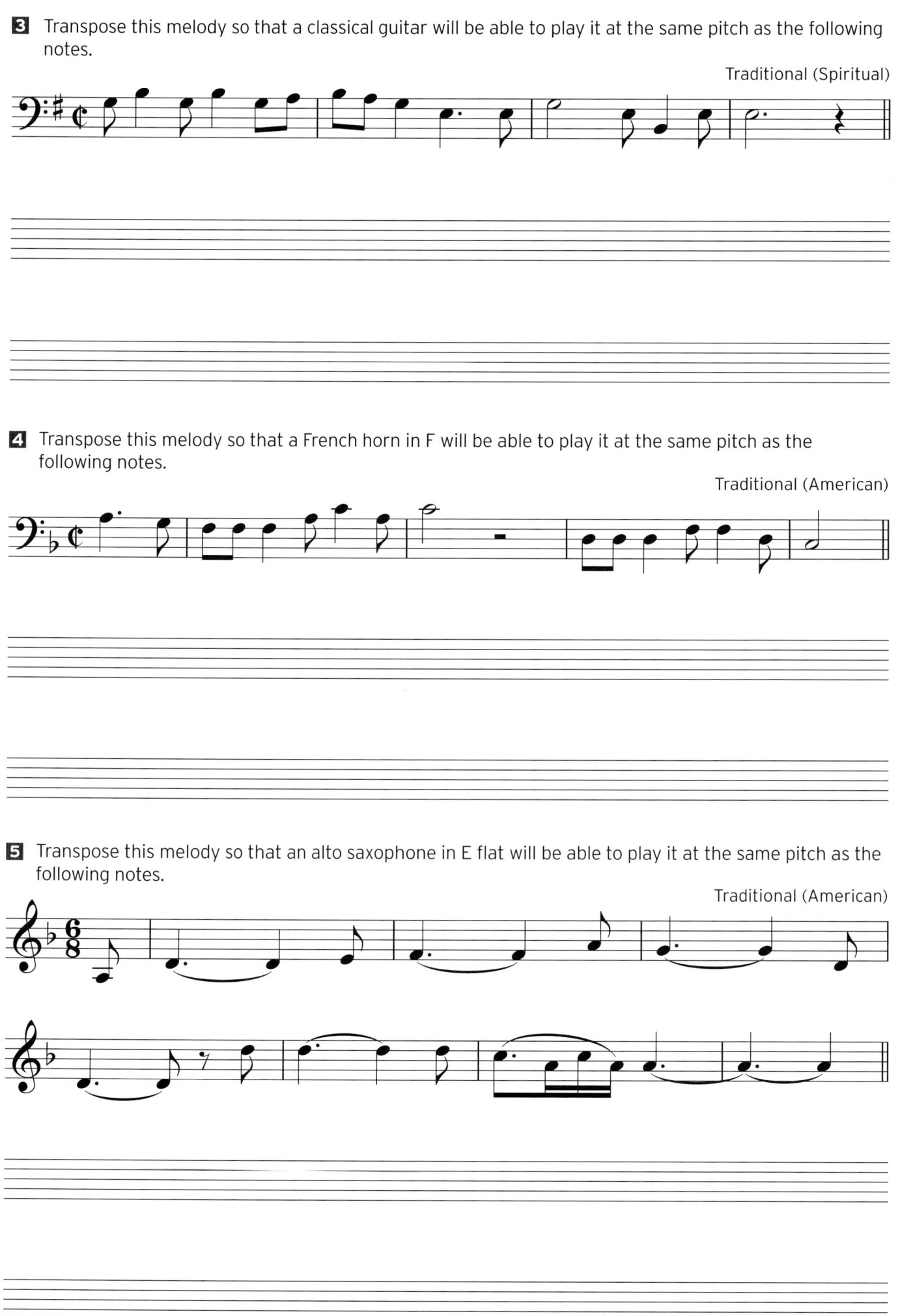

Mediant, submediant and leading note triads

In major keys

For Grade 6 you need to know every triad of the major scale.

Here is the scale of C major with triads built on every degree:

| 1 | 2 | 3 | 4 | 5 | 6 | 7 | 8(1) |
| tonic | supertonic | mediant | subdominant | dominant | submediant | leading note | tonic |

Look at the triads built on the 3rd, 6th and 7th degrees in the scale above:

The **mediant** triad is labelled iii or Em.

The **submediant** triad is labelled vi or Am.

The **leading note** triad is labelled vii or B° (or Bdim); both intervals of the triad are minor 3rds, making this a diminished triad (see page 40).

For Grade 6 you need to know that diminished triads do not have ° after them in the Roman numeral system. It is assumed that you know that some triads/chords in each key are diminished (or augmented; see page 37).

1 Here are some major scales. Write triads on every degree of the scale and label them with Roman numerals below the stave and chord symbols above.

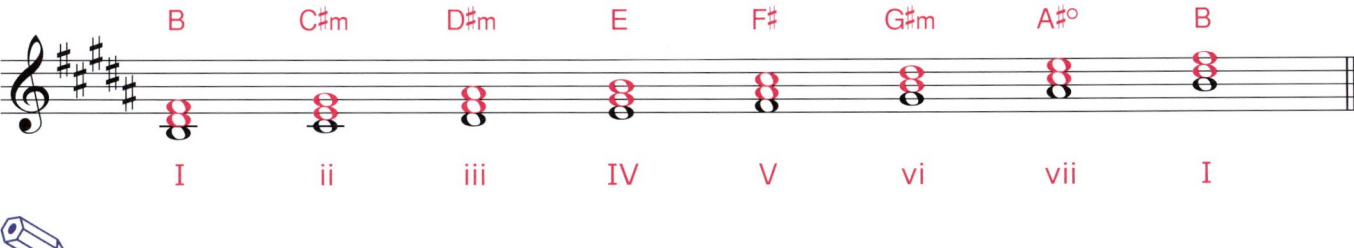

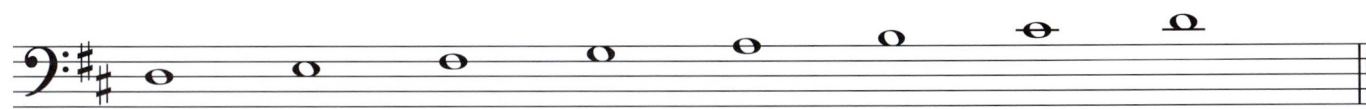

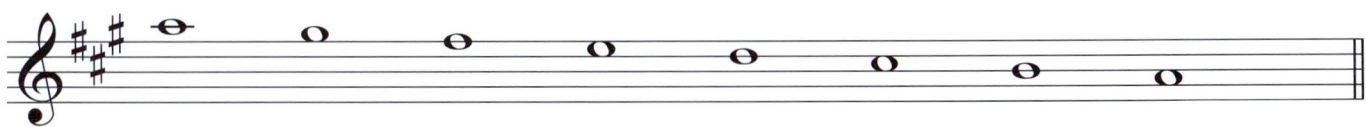

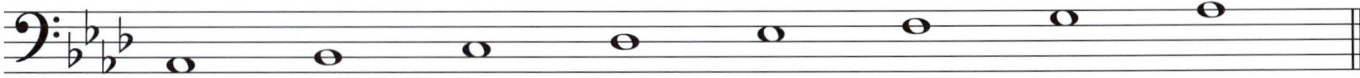

In minor keys

For Grade 6 you need to know every triad of the harmonic and melodic minor scales.

Here is the **harmonic minor scale of A minor** with triads built on every degree:

Look at the triads built on the 3rd, 6th and 7th degrees in the scale above:

The mediant triad is labelled III or C+; both intervals of the triad are major 3rds, making this an augmented triad.

The submediant triad is labelled VI or F.

The leading note triad is labelled vii or G♯° (or G♯dim); both intervals of the triad are minor 3rds, making this a diminished triad.

Here is the **melodic minor scale of A minor** with triads built on every degree:

Ascending, the triads differ from those of the harmonic scale only where the additional raised 6th degree makes the intervals in the triads change. Descending, the 6th and 7th degrees are lowered and the triads change accordingly.

Remember
The type of triad on each degree of a minor scale is the same for every harmonic or melodic minor scale.

1 Here are some harmonic and melodic minor scales. Write triads on every degree of the scale and label them with Roman numerals below the stave and chord symbols above.

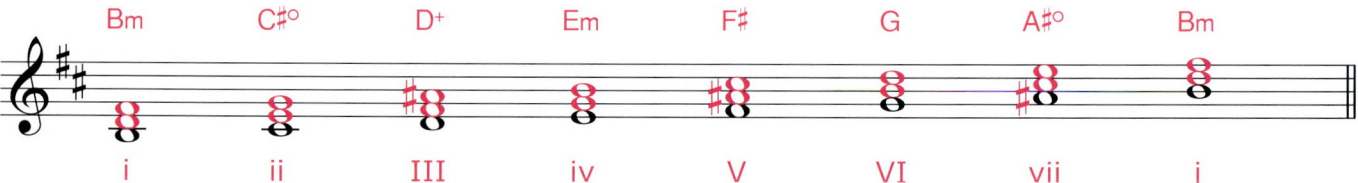

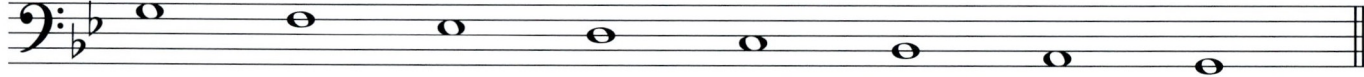

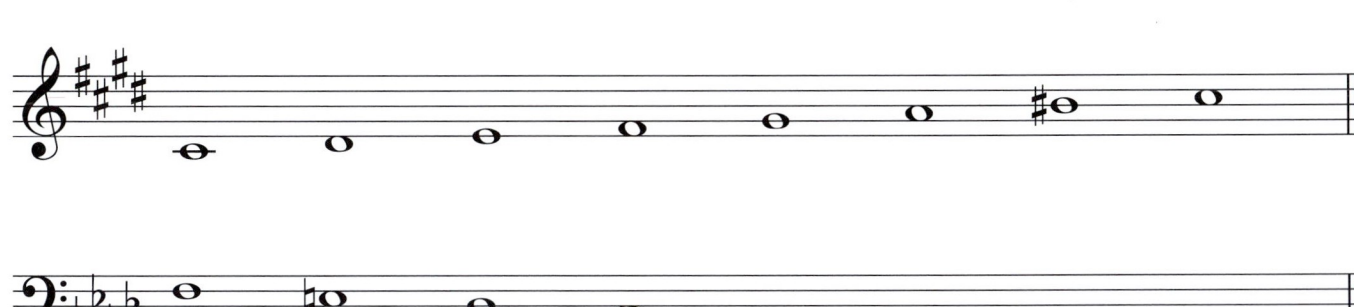

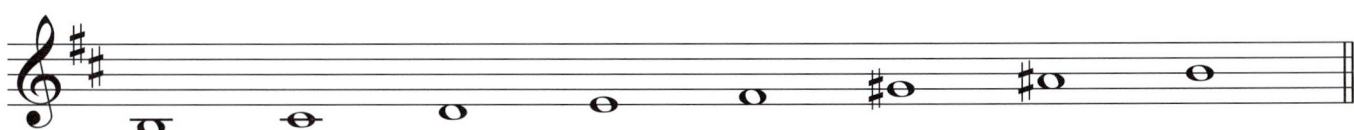

2 Label the chords with Roman numerals below the stave and chord symbols above.

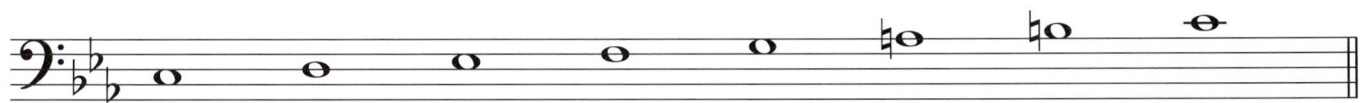

(C major)

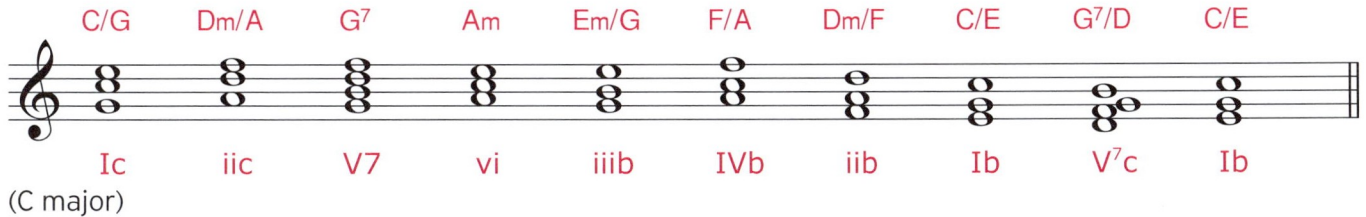

(B minor)

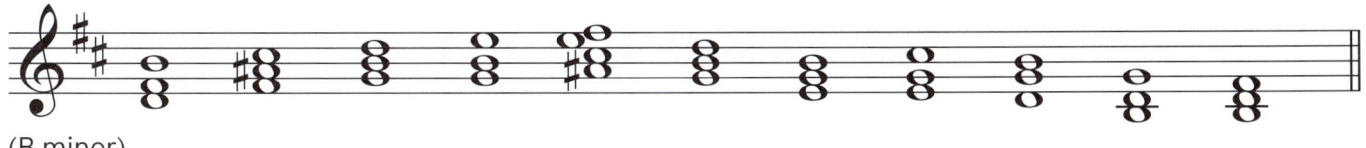

(G major)

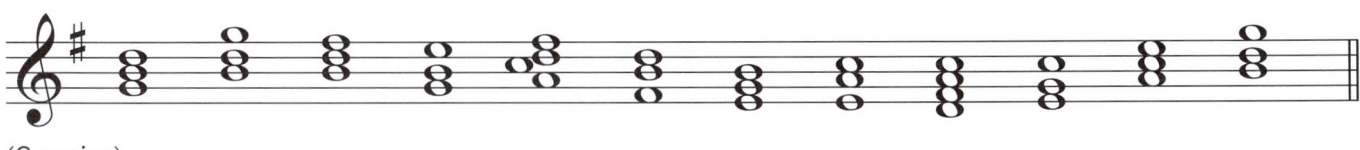

(E♭ major)

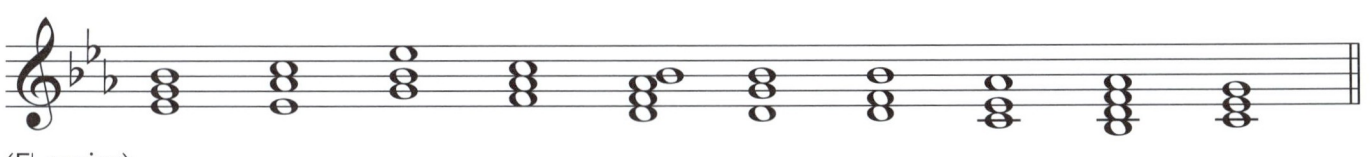

(F# minor)

Broken chords – dominant 7ths

As you know, a dominant 7th chord is built on the dominant triad of a key with a 7th added above its root.
For Grade 6 you need to know how to write broken chords using dominant 7th chords.

Remember
Composers use broken chords to give music different textures and to make accompaniments sound more interesting.

Here is the dominant 7th chord in C major and A minor:

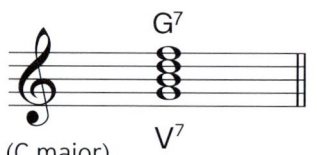
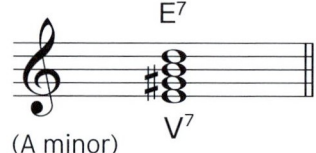

Remember
In minor keys, raise the pitch of the leading note of the key in V^7 chords (eg the G is raised to G♯ in A minor).

As with other broken chords composers use many different patterns. Here is one example showing a broken chord using the dominant 7th chord in A minor:

1 Using semiquavers, write broken chords using the appropriate chord. Use patterns of four notes each time. Finish no more than two leger lines above or below the stave.

V^7 in D minor descending

V^7 in C minor descending

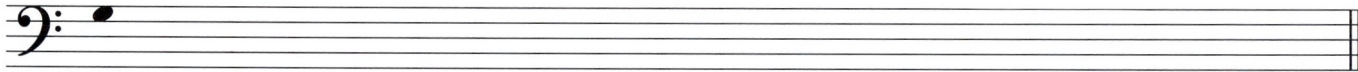

V^7 in E major descending

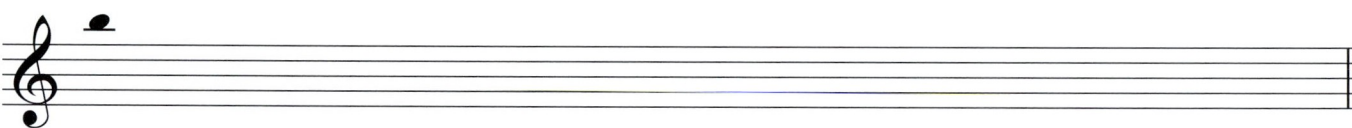

V^7 in A♭ major ascending

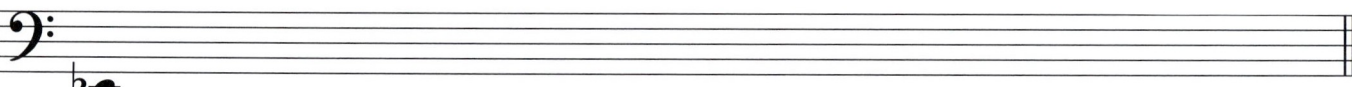

Diminished 7ths

 A **diminished 7th chord** is built on any diminished triad with a diminished 7th added above its root.

Here is a diminished triad on C: and a diminished 7th chord on C:

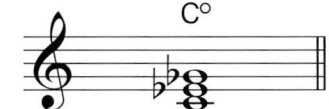 

Notice that there are minor 3rds between each interval of the diminished 7th chord:

Minor 3rd   Minor 3rd   Minor 3rd

The 'spelling' above is correct because there is a diminished 7th (**C-B♭♭**) between the bottom and top notes of the chord. However, in practice composers tend to use enharmonic equivalents instead:

Often these chords are written within a key signature so some accidentals are already included.

Did you know?
Diminished 7ths are unstable chords because they contain two tritones (written as diminished 5ths or augmented 4ths depending on the spelling). Composers often use these chords to add a sense of drama to the music.

Playlist: Diminished 7th Chords

- Mozart: Don Giovanni, K. 527, Act II: No. 24, Finale: c. Don Giovanni, a cenar teco (opening chord)
- Beethoven: Piano Sonata No. 18 in E♭ Major, Op. 31 No. 3 "The Hunt": I. Allegro (0:06)
- Benny Andersson, Björn Ulvaeus, Stig Anderson (ABBA): SOS (0:18)

1 Write intervals of a diminished 7th above these notes.

2 Write diminished 7th chords using the correct spelling. Then write the chord again, using enharmonic equivalents for the diminished 7ths.

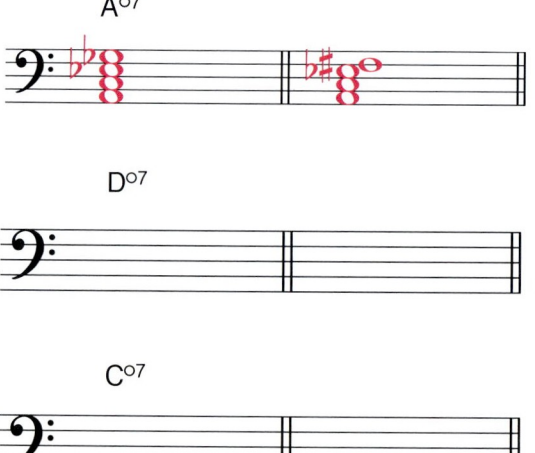

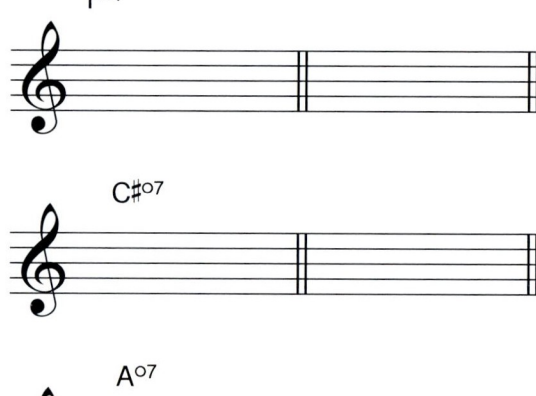

Broken chords - diminished 7ths

For Grade 6 you need to know how to write broken chords using diminished 7th chords.

1 Using semiquavers, write broken chords using the appropriate chord. Use patterns of four notes each time. Finish no more than two leger lines above or below the stave. Use the correct spelling.

Diminished 7th on D ascending

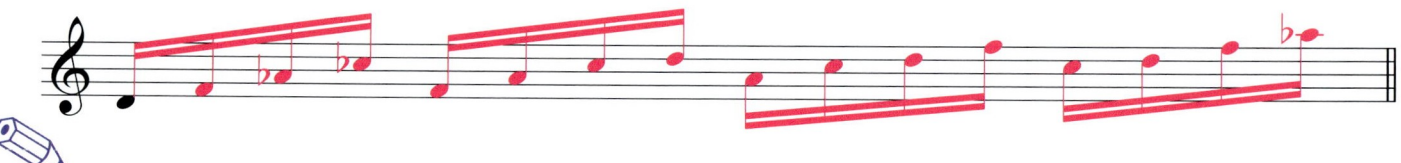

Diminished 7th on C descending

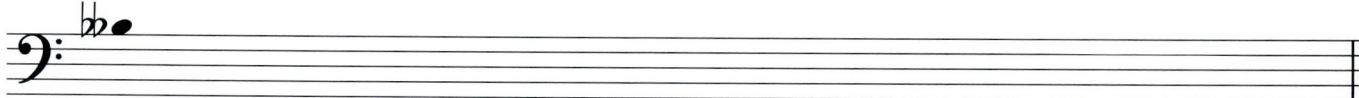

41

Diminished 7th on A ascending

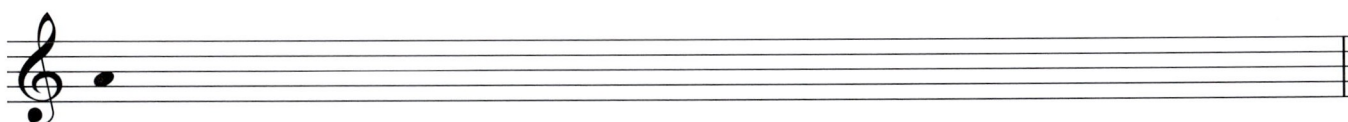

Diminished 7th on B♭ ascending

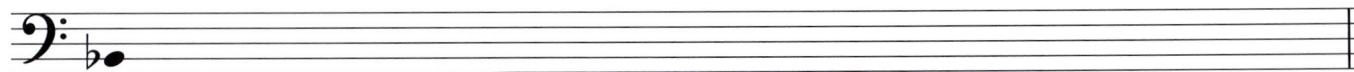

2 Write the following broken chords using note values of your choice. Use patterns of three or four notes each time. Finish no more than two leger lines above or below the stave.

Chord iii in D major descending, using a key signature

Chord V⁷ in F♯ minor ascending, without using a key signature

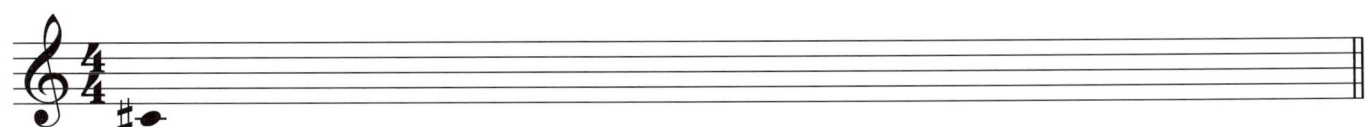

Chord iv in G minor descending, using a key signature

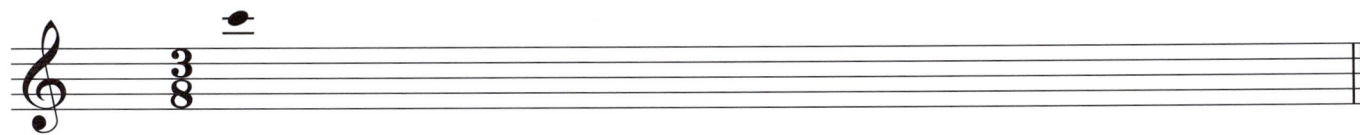

Chord G°⁷ ascending, without using a key signature (correct spelling)

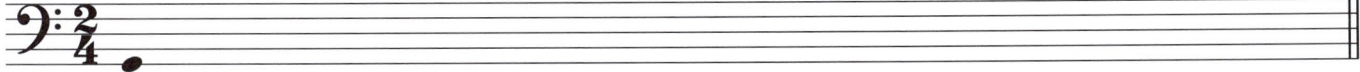

Compound intervals

Intervals larger than an octave are called **compound intervals**. For example, an octave plus a major 3rd can be called a compound major 3rd. You can also count the number from the bottom to the top and call it a major 10th.

Compound major 3rd (or major 10th)

For Grade 6 you need to name compound intervals.

1 Name the following intervals in two ways, as shown above.

36

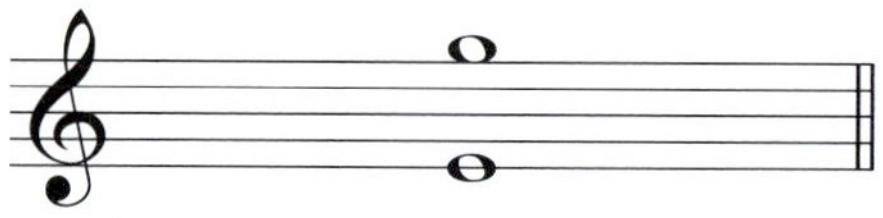

Interval: _____

or: _____

37

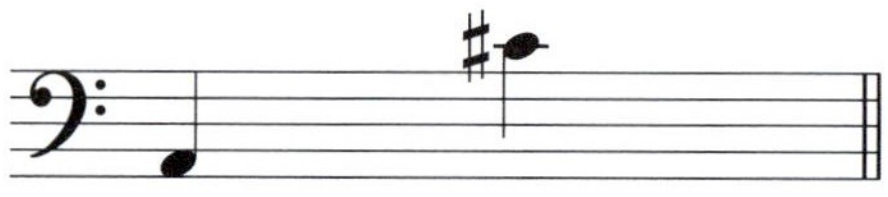

Interval: _____

or: _____

38

Interval: _____

or: _____

39

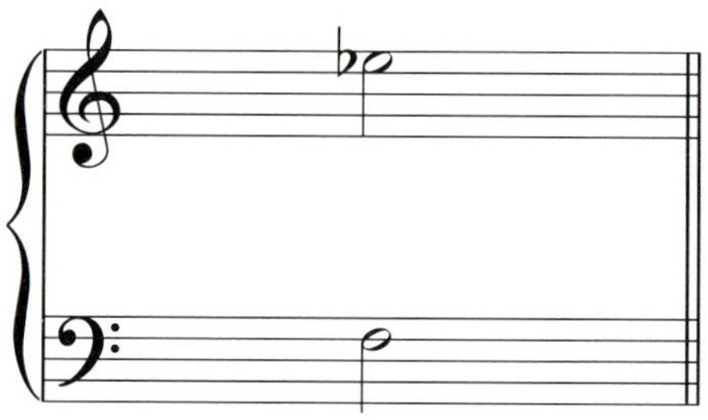

Interval: _____

or: _____

40

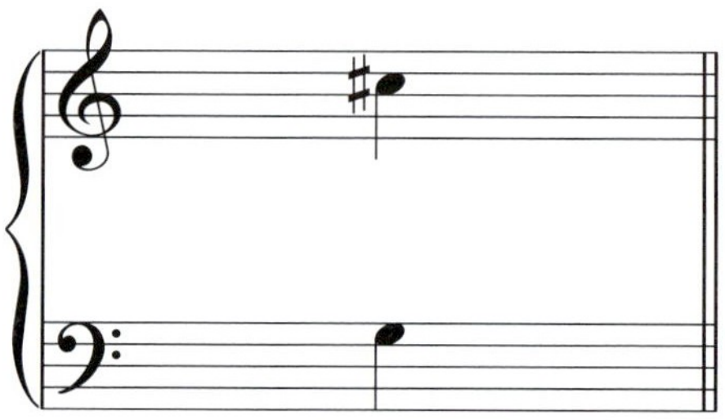

Interval: _____

or: _____

41

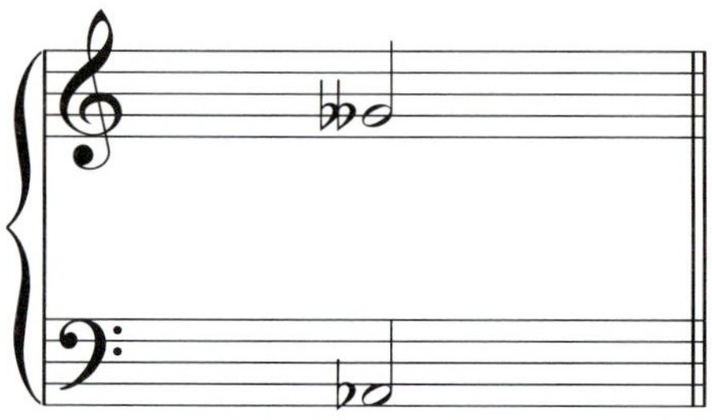

Interval: _____

or: _____

42

Interval: _____

or: _____

43

Interval: _____

or: _____

44

Interval: _____

or: _____

2 Name the following intervals. Where the intervals are compound, label them using one of the two possible names.

Interval: **Minor 7th**

Interval: _____

Interval: _____

Interval: _____

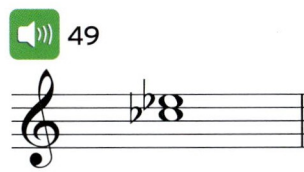

Interval: _____

Interval: _____

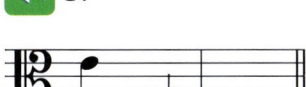

Interval: _____

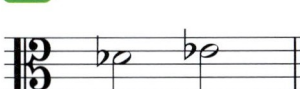

Interval: _____

Interval: _____

Interval: _____

Interval: _____

Interval: _____

Interval: _____

Interval: _____

Interval: _____

Interval: _____

Interval: _____

Interval: _____

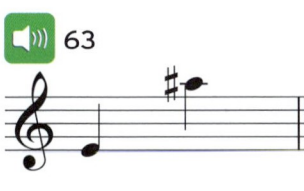

Interval: _____

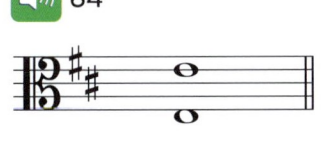

Interval: _____

Interval: _____

Figured bass

Figured bass (used a lot in Baroque music, see page 65) is a system designed to indicate which chords to play by referring to the interval number between a) the bass and middle notes and, b) the bass and top notes of the chord when written as a triad.

Here is a tonic triad in C major shown in root, first and second inversion, labelled with figured bass.

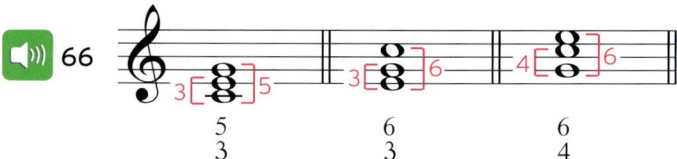

The keyboard (or continuo) player would see only the bass line and figures below, from this they would be able to improvise in the style of the music; just as a jazz musician would improvise from chords. Here is a tonic chord in C major for SATB shown in root, first and second inversion, labelled with figured bass. Notice the way compound intervals are used.

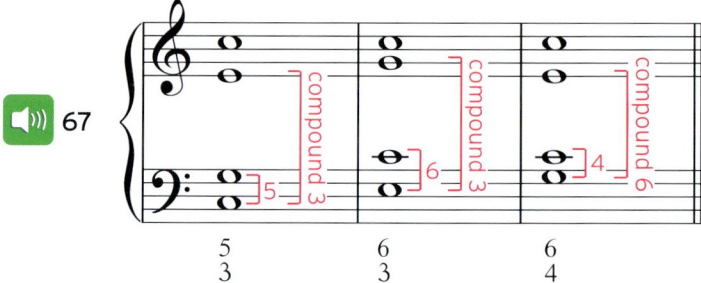

Reading and improvising from a figured bass was a highly refined art in the Baroque period and all continuo players would have been fully familiar with it. In more modern editions, **realisations** of the figured bass are usually written out for the player, but this is just one way of interpreting the music.

For Grade 6 you only need to know figured bass for major and minor chords in root, first and second inversion.

Did you know?

In the figured bass system, where no number is written below a bass note, the composer wants the continuo player to play a chord in root position. If there is just an accidental below a bass note, this means that a root position chord is intended but that the 3rd of the chord is to be altered using that accidental. For example:

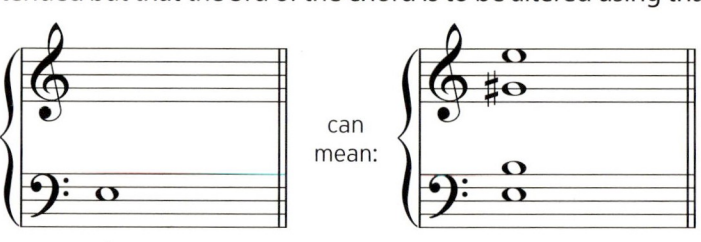

can mean:

(or a chord with the same notes at different registers; though the bass note is fixed)

Where just a 6 appears below a chord, this means that a first inversion chord is intended.

1 Write the key signature and the tonic triad in root, first or second inversion for each key shown.

(G# minor) 6/3   (G# minor)   (G# minor) 6/4

(A major) 6/4   (A major) 6   (A major)

(B♭ major)   (B♭ major) 6/4   (B♭ major) 6

(G minor) 6/3   (G minor)   (G minor) 6/4

> **Did you know?**
> Second inversion chords written for SATB double the fifth of the chord, not the root.

2 Write the key signature for the key shown. Using crotchets, write out 4-part tonic chords for SATB in either root, first or second inversion, as shown by the figured bass.

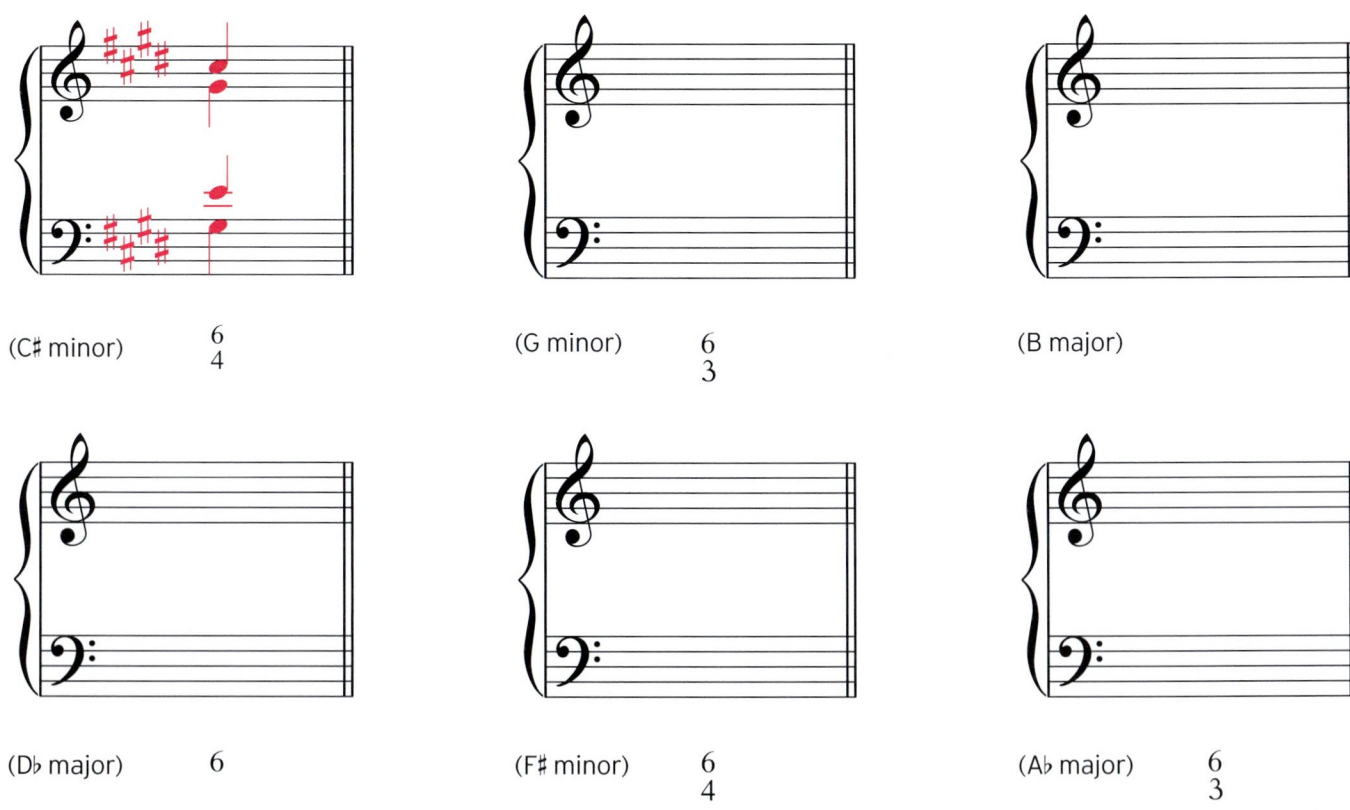

(C# minor) 6/4   (G minor) 6/3   (B major)

(D♭ major) 6   (F# minor) 6/4   (A♭ major) 6/3

4-part chords

For Grade 6 you need to write any chord (major, minor, diminished, augmented, dominant 7th or diminished 7th) for SATB (from Roman numerals or chord symbols) in root position or in inversion.

As you will probably already know, when writing for SATB (or four instrumental parts), chords in root position or first inversion will often double the root note, whilst in second inversion it is usual to double the fifth. Sometimes, composers leave out the fifth of a chord.

Dominant and diminished 7th chords have four different notes so, strictly speaking, it is not necessary to double any of the notes when writing for SATB.

1 Circle the root(s) in the following chords and label each with a Roman numeral below and a chord symbol above. Diminished chords are spelt correctly.

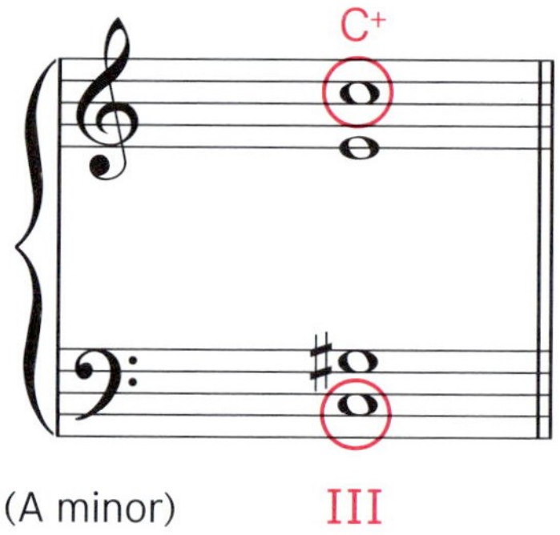

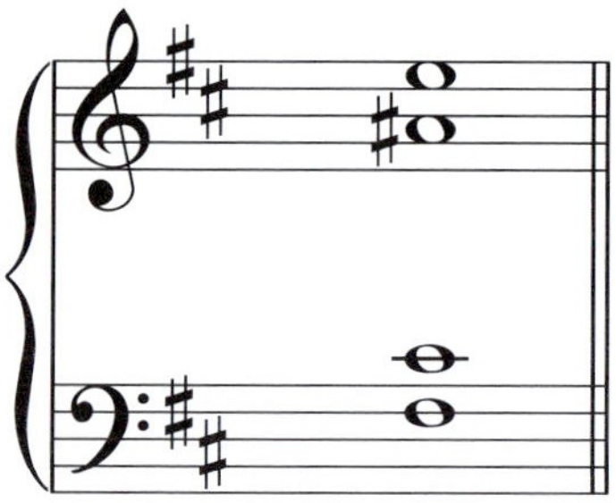

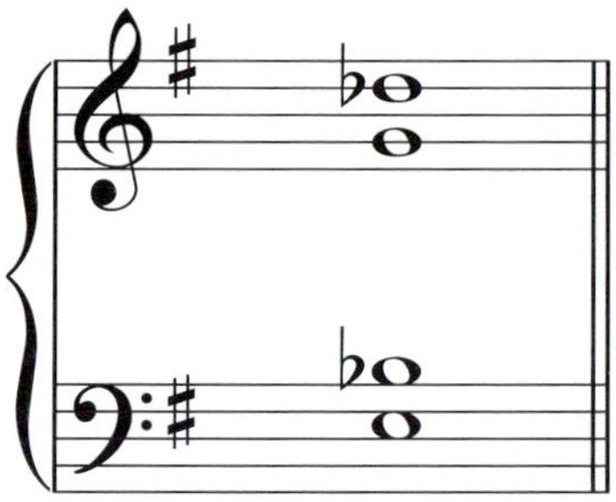

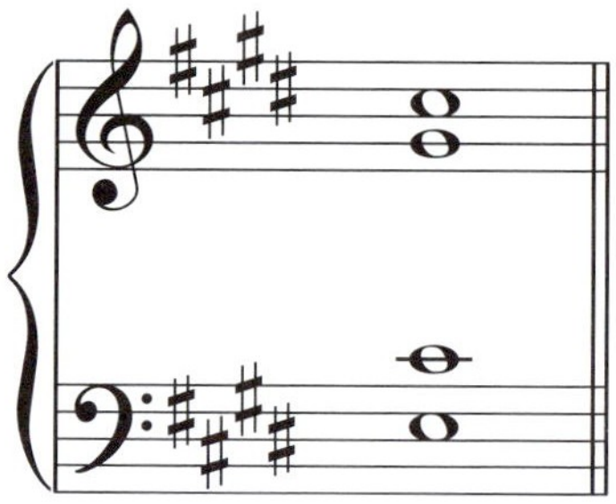

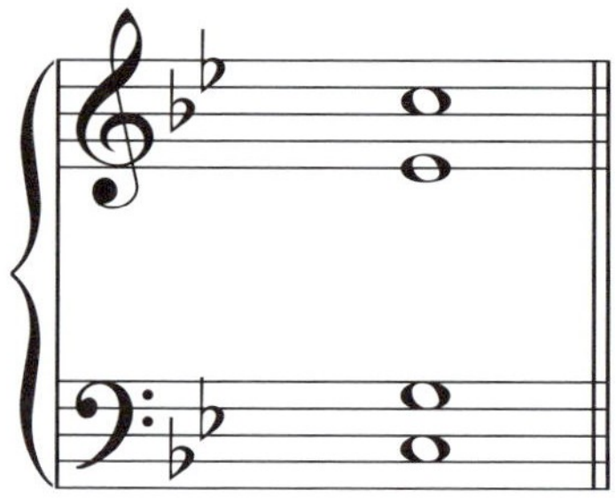

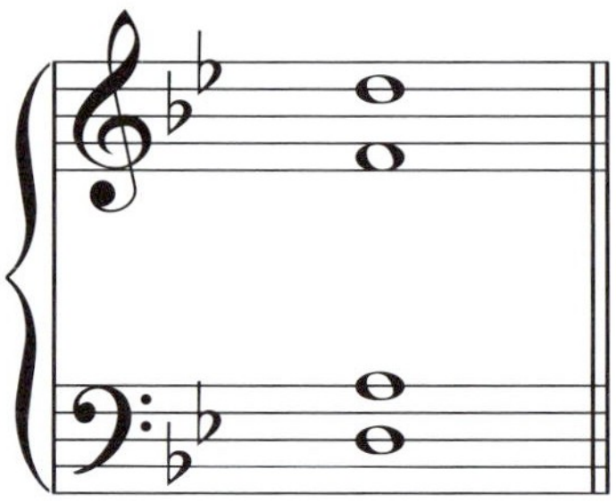

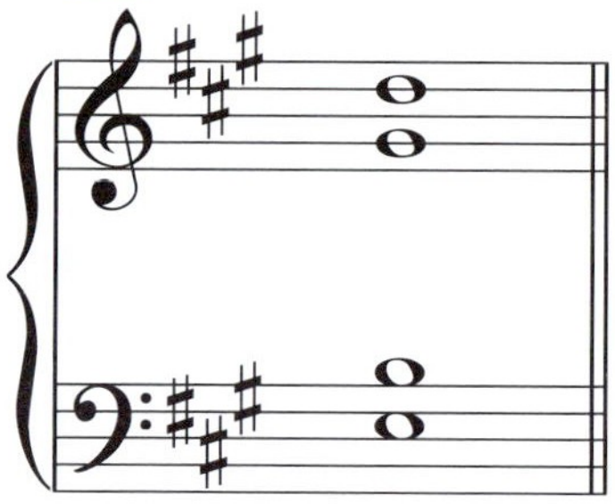

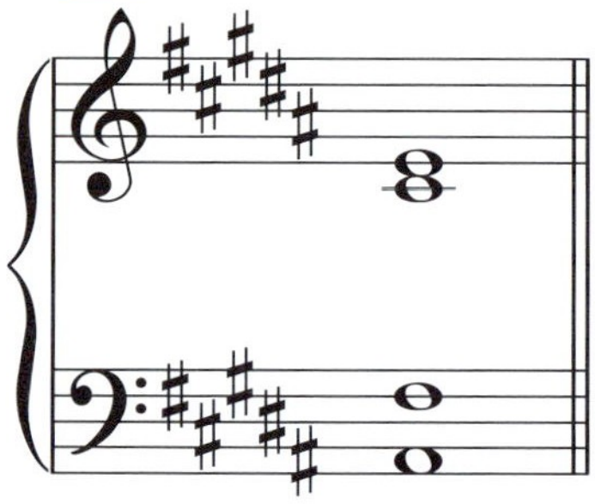

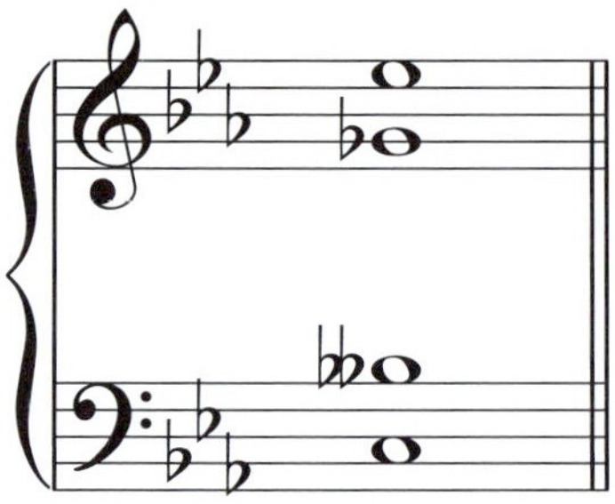

2 Using crotchets, write out 4-part chords for SATB using the chords shown by the Roman numerals. Then write an appropriate chord symbol above.

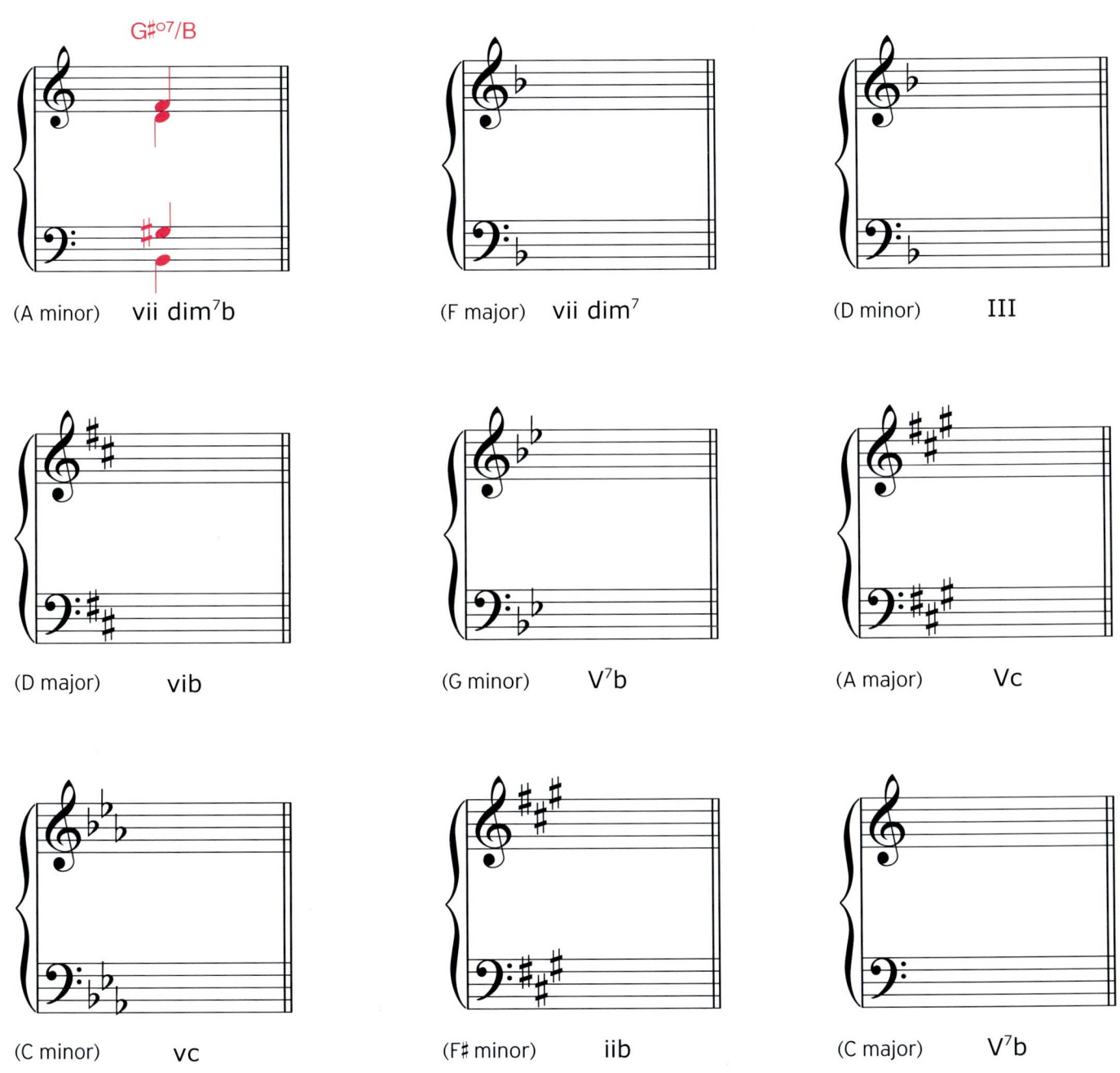

Handy tip!
Dominant and diminished 7th chords may appear in 3rd inversion. If this is the case, you will see **d** written after the Roman numeral given.

Remember
In minor keys, check the Roman numerals to see whether the 3rd of the chord should be raised.

Close and open scores

Here is one phrase of a chorale (see page 71) written on two staves for SATB, in **close score** (all parts written on two staves):

Close score

J S Bach

For Grade 6 you need to be able to transfer a phrase like this for SATB from close score to open score and vice versa. **Open score** is where each part is written on a separate stave.

> ### Did you know?
> Composers often copy music by other composers to get a feel for the way music is put together. As you transfer the music to open score (or vice versa) notice how the individual voice parts move and how the composer invents good chord progressions.

To transfer to open score: write each part on a separate stave, using stems as you would if you were writing for one part only. Here is the above example written in open score:

Open score

J S Bach

> ### Remember
> In open score, music for tenor voice is written in treble clef an octave higher than it sounds. It is shown here in the coloured box.
>
> Often there is a figure 8 below the clef – to show the octave transposition.

To transfer to close score: Do the opposite.

NB The note heads are aligned vertically so that the beats line up.

> ### Handy tip!
> Use a ruler for bar lines.

1 Transfer these chorale phrases to open score.

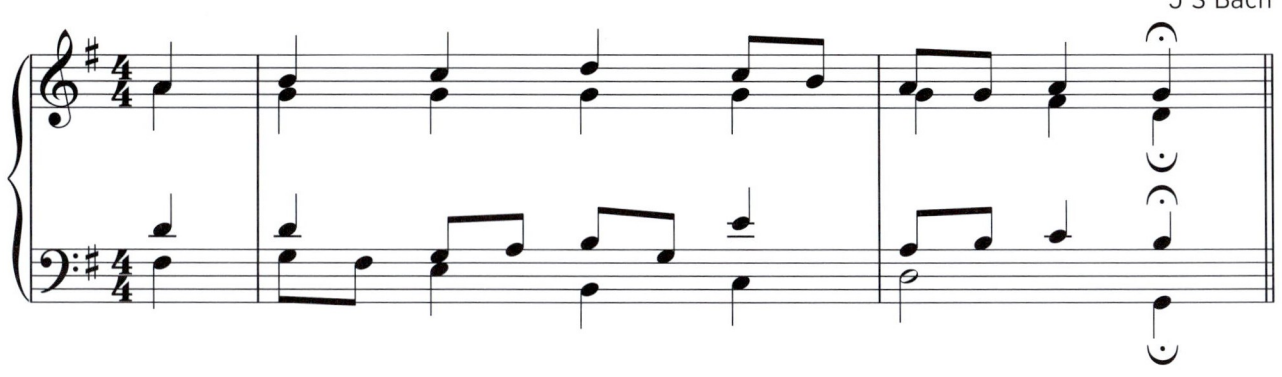

J S Bach

J S Bach

2 Transfer these chorale phrases to close score.

J S Bach

J S Bach

3 Circle any passing notes in the chorale phrases above. Mark any accented passing notes with **APN** above the circle. Put a cross above any auxiliary notes (for explanations, see Grade 5 workbook).

Cadences

More imperfect cadences

So far you have learned to recognise perfect, plagal and some imperfect cadences approached from the tonic and the supertonic. Here are examples of the new types of **imperfect cadences** that you need to know for Grade 6.

Approached from the subdominant:

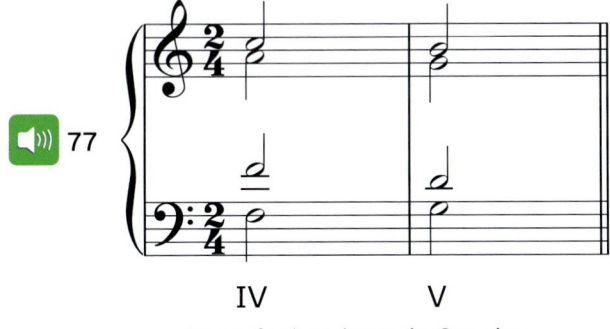

IV   V
Imperfect cadence in C major

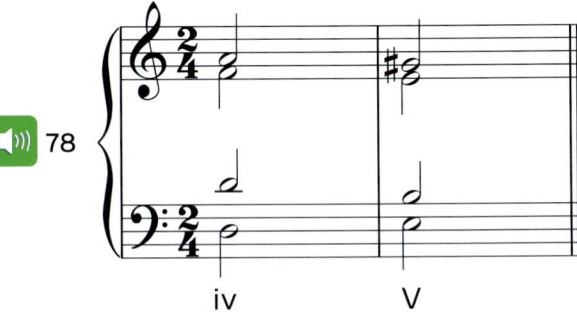

iv   V
Imperfect cadence in A minor

Approached from the submediant:

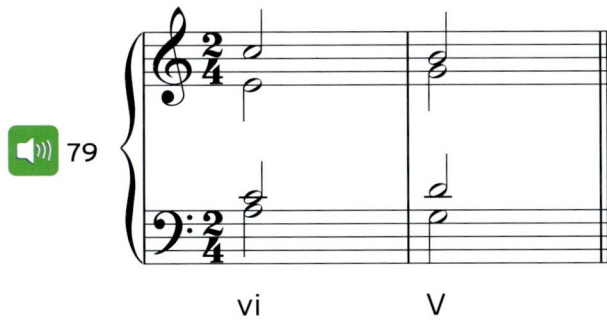

vi   V
Imperfect cadence in C major

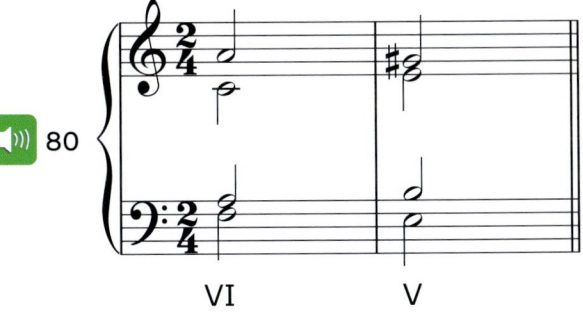

VI   V
Imperfect cadence in A minor

Approached from the tonic (second inversion):

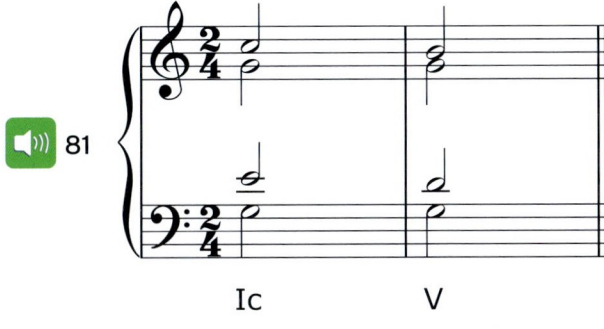

Ic   V
Imperfect cadence in C major

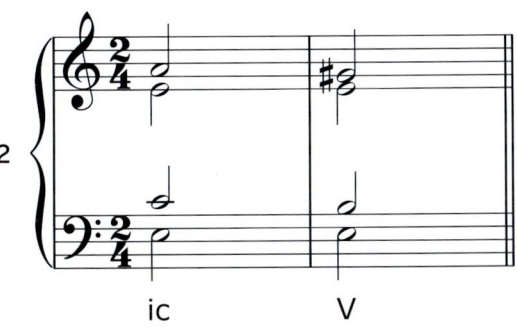

ic   V
Imperfect cadence in A minor

Remember
Imperfect cadences close on the dominant chord, not the tonic. They are also known as half closes. Like all cadences, they are often decorated.

Playlist: Imperfect Cadences

- Beethoven: Piano Concerto No. 4 in G Major, Op. 58: I. Allegro moderato (0:20)

The interrupted cadence

Play the following cadences to hear why they are called interrupted cadences. The listener hears the dominant (or dominant 7th) chord and expects a perfect cadence; instead the submediant chord is played and it comes as a surprise.

Here are some examples:

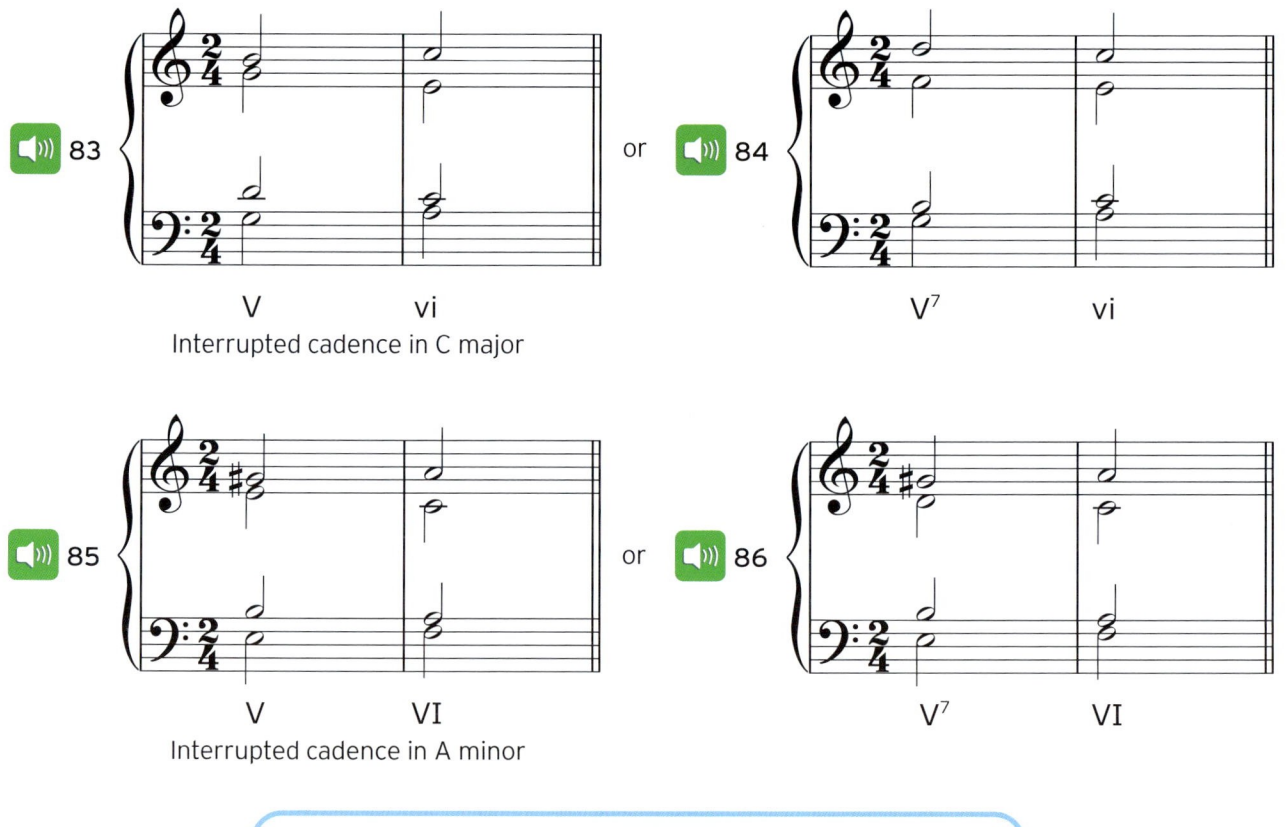

Handy tip!
To avoid parallel 5ths and octaves in this cadence, the 3rd is sometimes doubled in chord vi or VI, when writing for SATB.

Playlist: Interrupted Cadences

- Mozart: Piano Sonata No. 3 in B♭ Major, K. 281: II. Andante amoroso (1:15- 1:18)
- Prokofiev: Symphony No. 1 in D Major, Op. 25 – "Classical": III. Gavotta, Non troppo allegro (0:07-0:08)
- Roger Waters (Pink Floyd): Bring the Boys Back Home (0:46-0:48)

> **Remember**
> Composers often decorate cadences and they do not always write all the notes of the chords that they are using. Look at the key signature, bass line and any accidentals to work out the type of cadence and the key.

NB In contrast to writing for SATB, composers may sometimes include parallel octaves when writing for keyboard/piano.

1 Look at these cadences. Give the key and say which type of cadence it is. Label the chords with Roman numerals below the stave and chord symbols above.

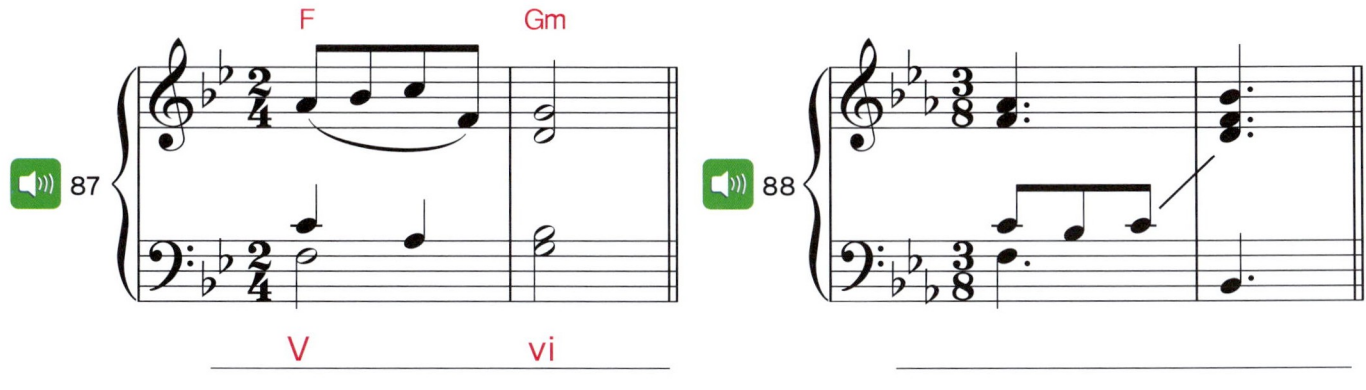

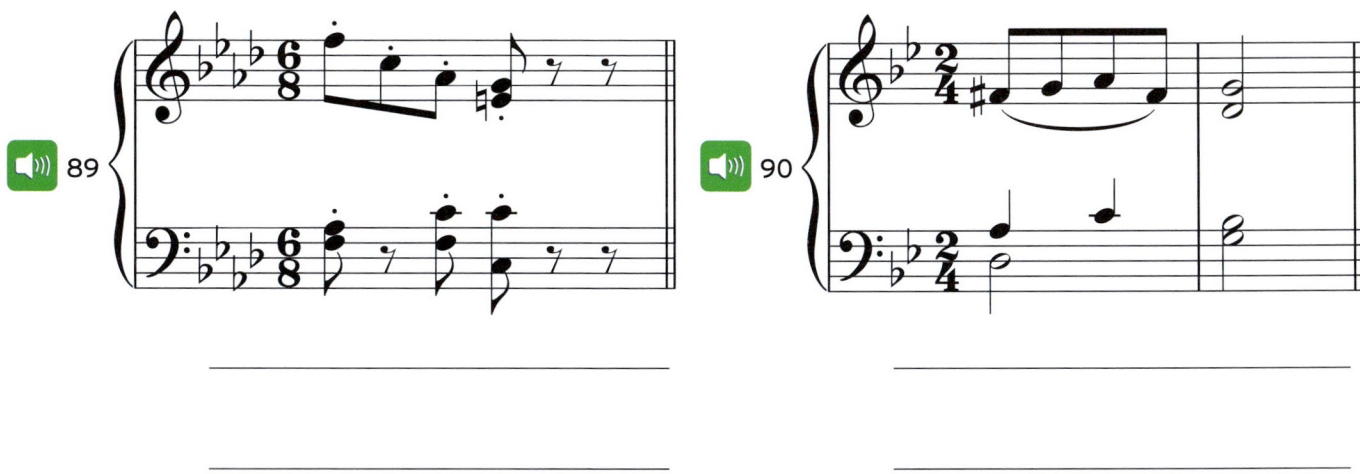

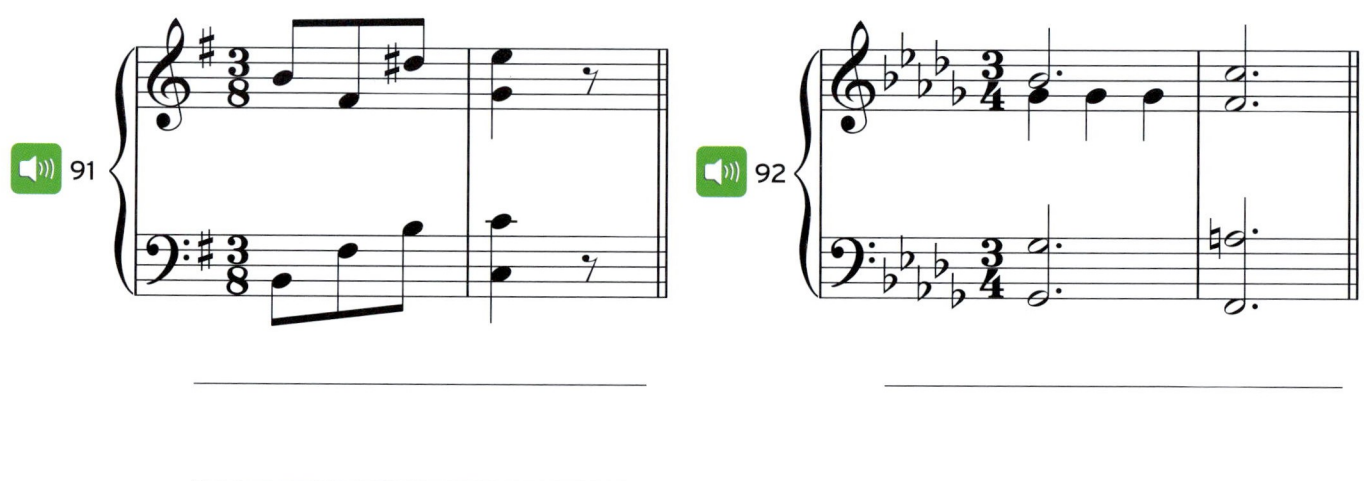
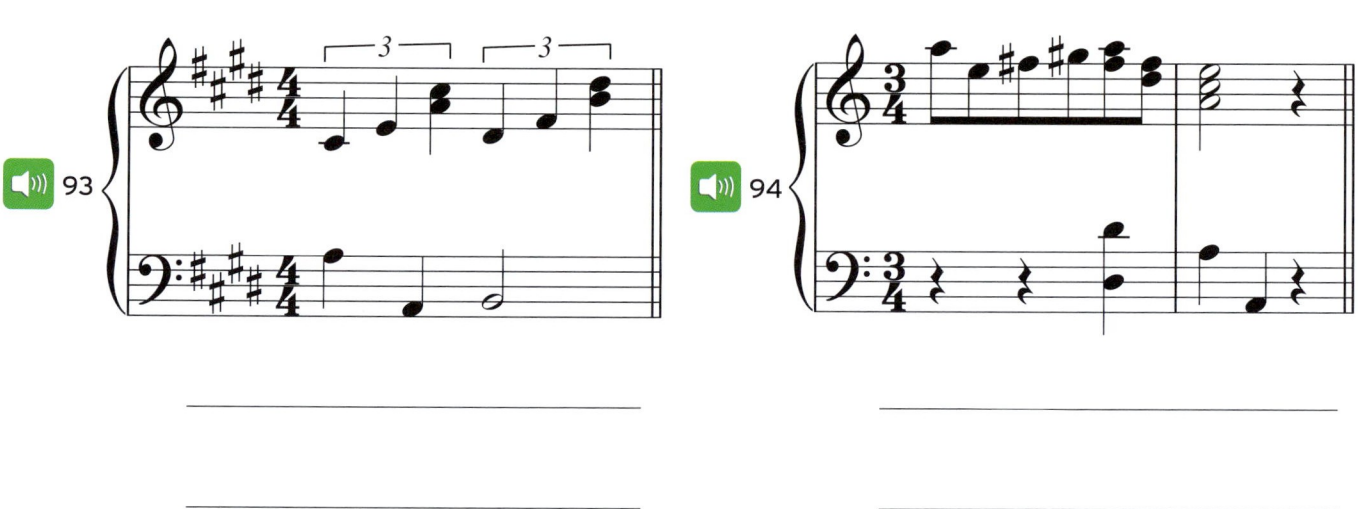
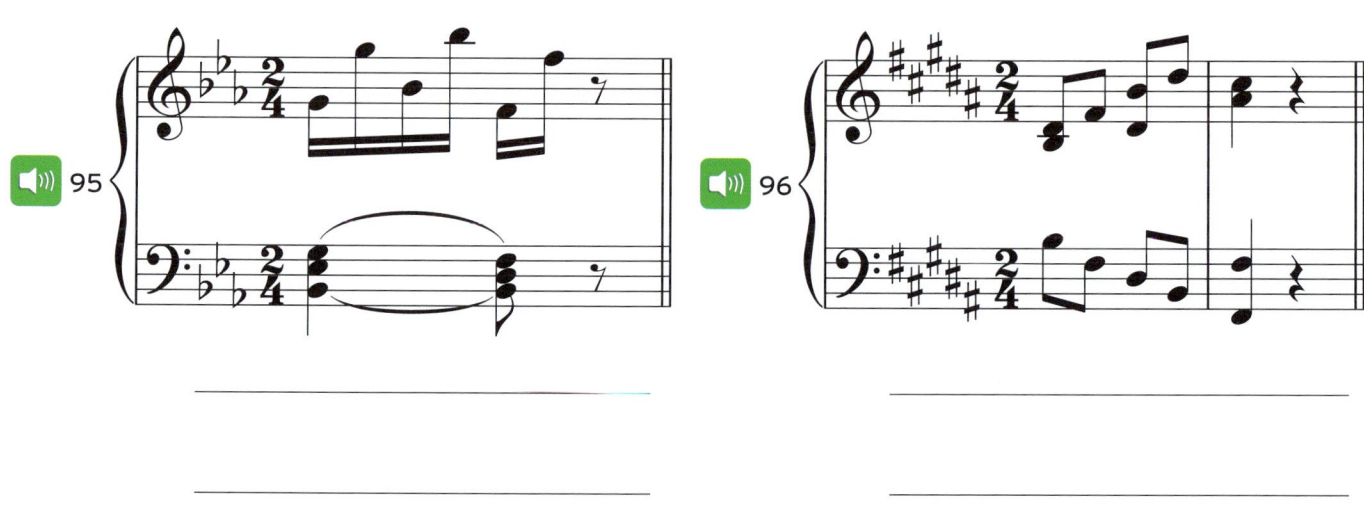

Writing 4-part cadences for SATB

 For Grade 6 you need to be able to label chords of a chorale or hymn phrase with Roman numerals and chord symbols; also to complete it with an appropriate cadence for SATB.

Remember
When completing the cadences, write smoothly for each voice part and include passing notes where appropriate. The 6th degree of the scale is often raised in minor keys where the ascending melodic scale is used so that the contour of the voice part moves smoothly up to the leading note.

Remember
Do not let any voices move in similar motion in perfect 5ths or octaves; this sounds weak and will lose you marks in your exam.

Handy tip!
Play or listen to chorales and hymns, and notice the chord progressions, especially at cadence points.

1 Label the chords of each phrase with Roman numerals below the stave and chord symbols above and complete it with an appropriate cadence.

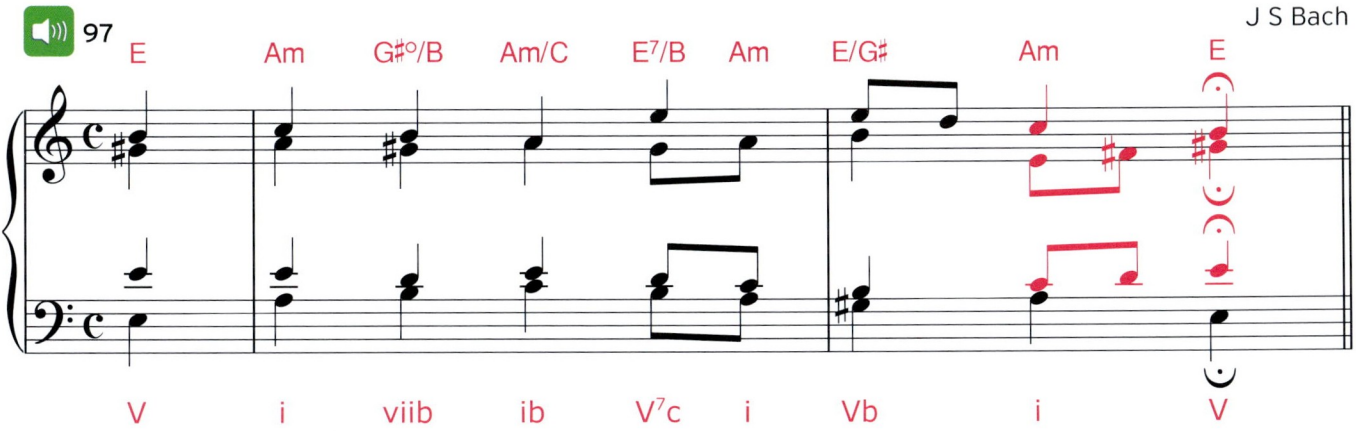

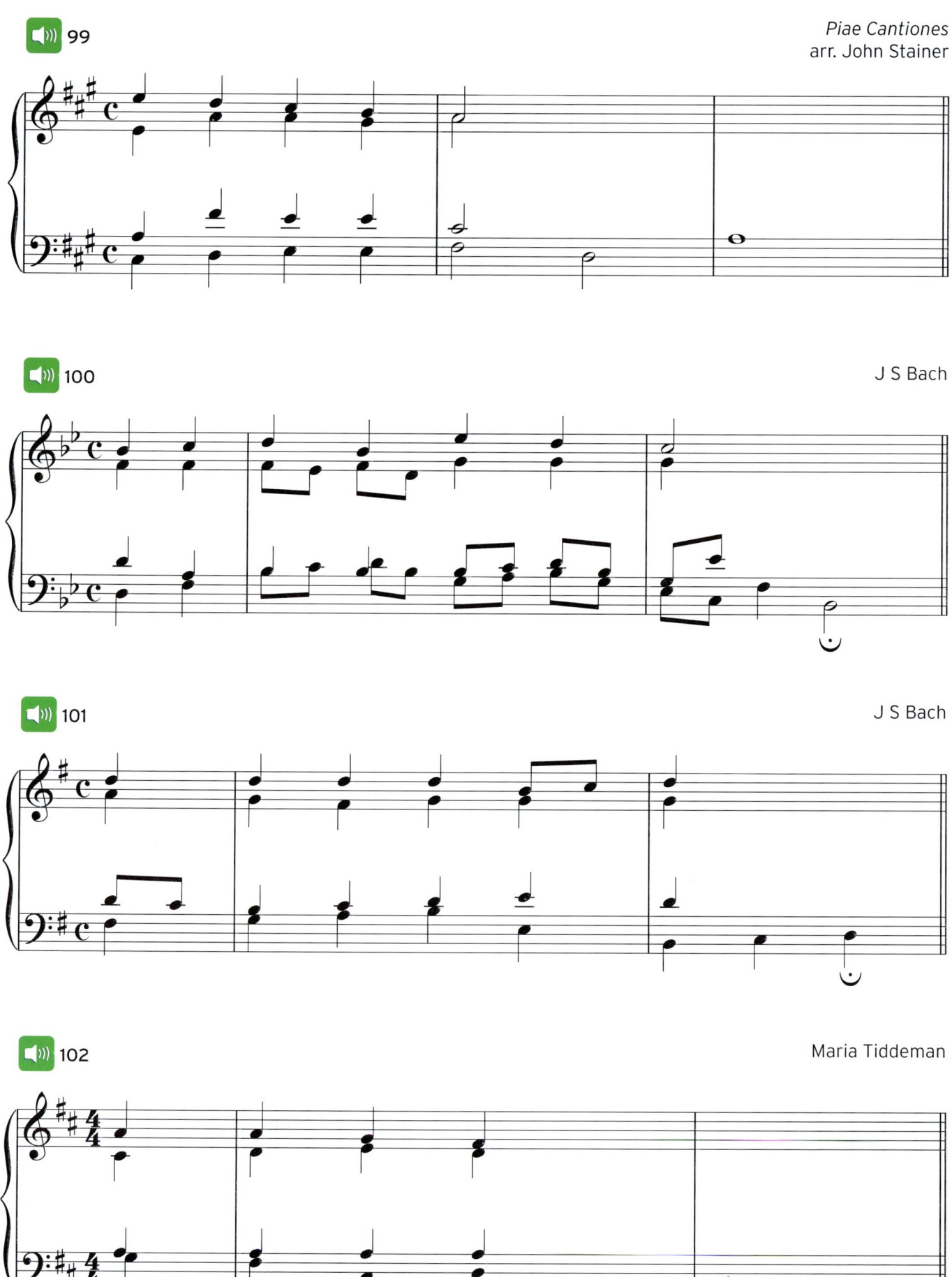

Harmonic sequences

A melodic sequence is a tune pattern that is repeated starting on a different note. A **harmonic sequence** is a chord pattern that is repeated at a different pitch (often it has a melodic sequence above it, but not always). Harmonic sequences are often used by composers; for Grade 6 you need to be able to recognise them in a piece of music.

Here are harmonic sequences shown in the coloured boxes, in C major then A minor:

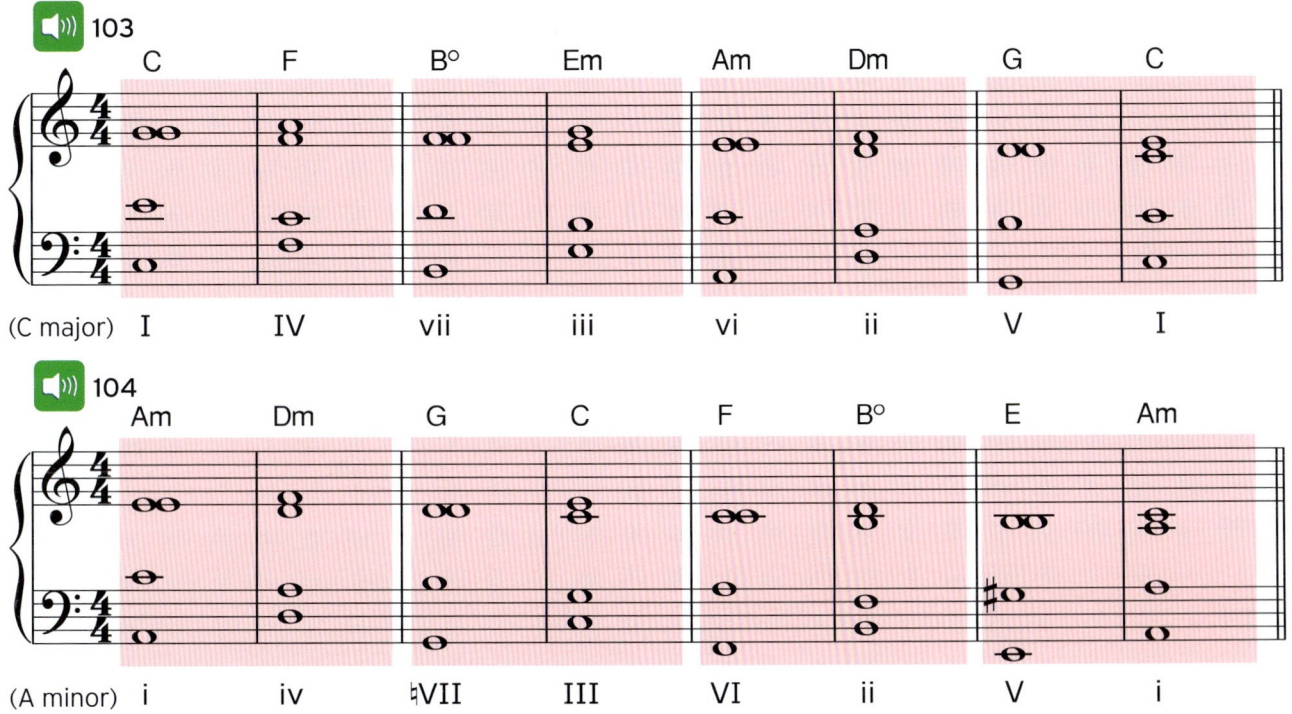

NB: Play the harmonic sequence in A minor. Because the movement of the sequence is downwards, the notes of A melodic minor have been used to keep a smooth contour in the part-writing, except for the perfect cadence at the end. Here are similar harmonic sequences in C major then A minor. This time first inversion chords are used between those in root position:

Baroque composers use these types of sequences often; especially in the B section of binary-form movements (see page 65). If the sequences are altered chromatically, they are an effective way to travel through different keys back to the tonic. Here is a melodic sequence in the recorder line with a downward harmonic sequence accompanying it. Notice that the sequence is decorated and chromatically altered, but that it is a version of the kind of sequences shown on page 58.

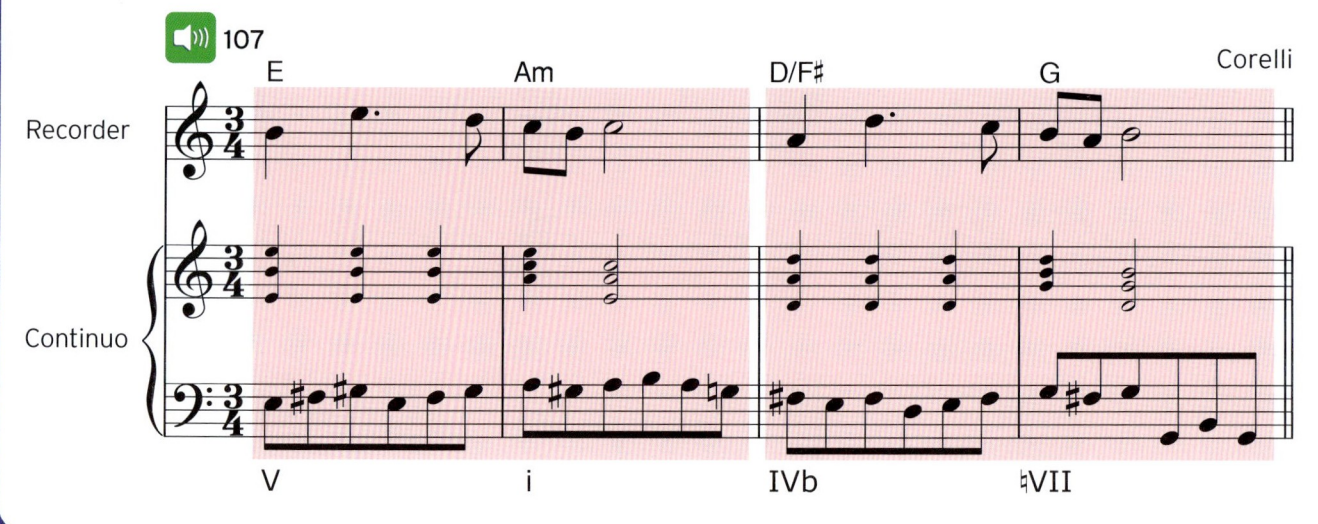

Handy tip!
Harmonic sequences can move upwards or downwards.

1 Bracket the harmonic sequences in this music.

a

b 109

Corelli

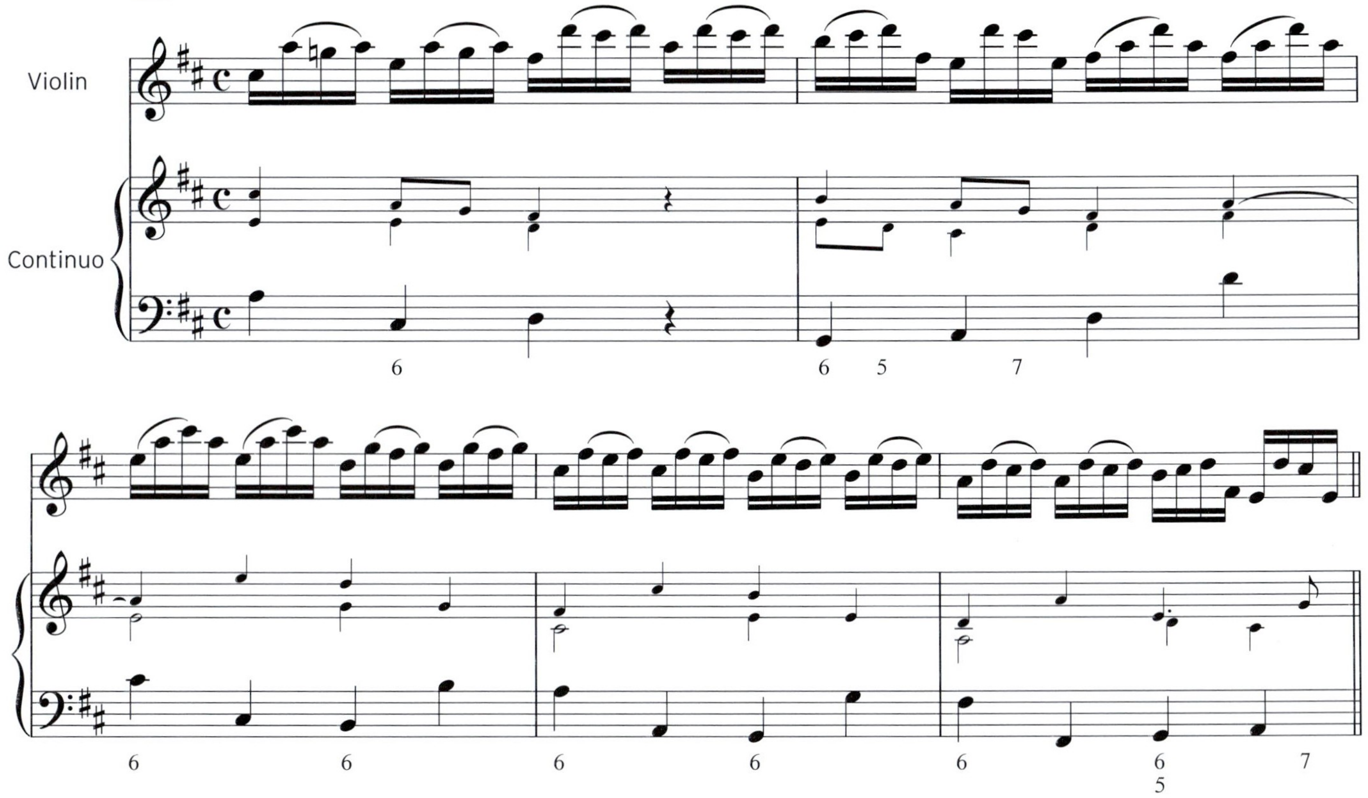

c 110

Telemann

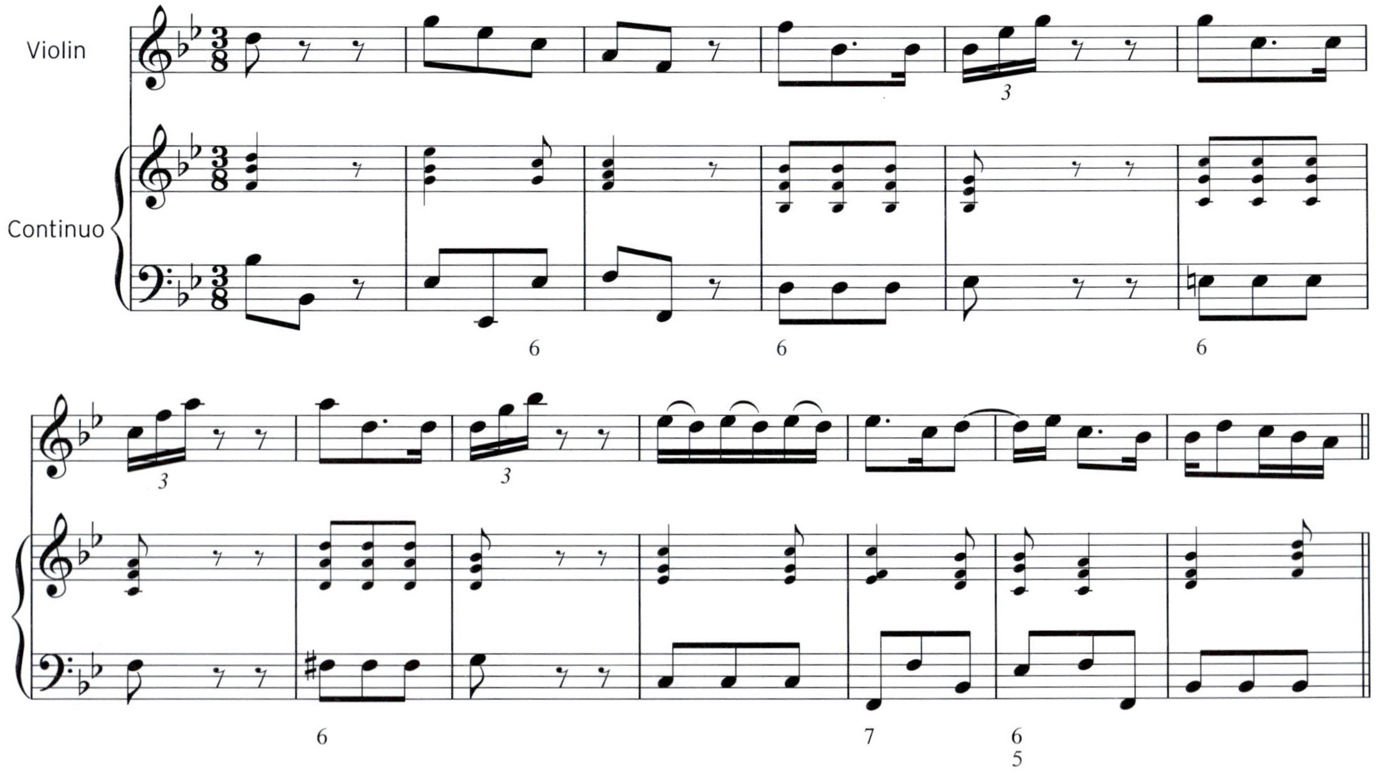

d 🔊 111

Vivaldi

2. Here are some chord progressions. Make each into a harmonic sequence by repeating it one note lower to complete the phrase.

a

(A major)

Texture

Texture is a word that musicians use to describe the fabric of the music; whether the parts move together or weave around independently, and whether the texture feels thick or thin. The type of instruments or voices (and the register at which they are playing or singing) influences the texture of music.

For Grade 6 you need to know these words to describe the texture of music:

Homophonic - all parts moving in the same rhythm

Handel

Polyphonic – two or more parts weaving around one another independently (usually meeting at cadence points)

J S Bach

> **Did you know?**
> Music may be said to be **imitative** if the parts copy one another exactly or partially.

The following words may be used to describe texture in music (homophonic or polyphonic):

Thick or **dense** – instrument(s) or voices playing or singing (often at a low register) with closely spaced chords, usually with many parts.

Thin or **transparent** – instrument(s) or voices playing or singing (often far apart in register), usually with few parts. This makes it easy to hear individual lines.

Here is an example where thick and thin textures are contrasted. The dynamics help create the textures too:

Beethoven

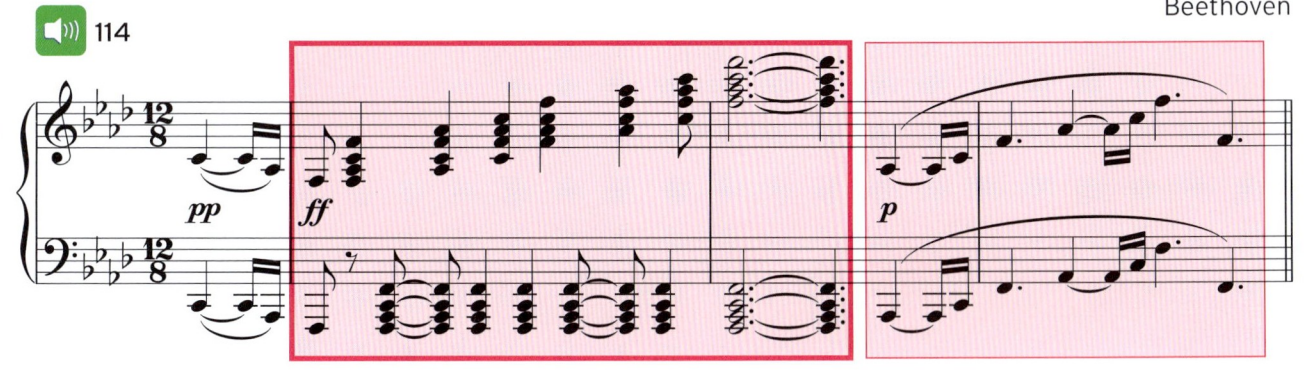

Playlist: Texture

Homophonic:
- Bach: Ach Gott und Herr, BWV 255
- Handel: Messiah, HWV 56, Pt. 2: No. 33, Chorus. Lift Up Your Heads, O Ye Gates
- Freddie Mercury (Queen): Bohemian Rhapsody

Polyphonic:
- Palestrina: Masses, Book 5: Missa Aeterna Christi munera: Sanctus
- Mozart: Requiem, K. 626: II. Kyrie
- Louise Farrenc: 30 Piano études, Op. 26: No. 12 in E Major, Moderato. Fuga a due Soggetti
- Shostakovich: Symphony No. 5 in D Minor, Op. 47: I. Moderato

Thick or dense texture:
- Richard Strauss: Don Juan, Op. 20
- Brahms: Symphony No. 4 in E Minor, Op. 98: III. Allegro giocoso – Poco meno presto – Tempo I
- Orff: Carmina Burana: XXV. O Fortuna

Thin or transparent texture:
- Arvo Pärt: Spiegel im Spiegel
- John Tavener: The Protecting Veil: I. The Protecting Veil
- John Williams: Hedwig's Theme (from Harry Potter and the Philosopher's Stone)

Musical words and symbols

Form

From Grade 5 you know about **binary form** (sometimes known as AB structure because it has two sections). Many pieces in binary form were written in the Baroque period (approximately 1600–1750) and the character of the pieces was often inspired by the rhythms and dance moves of popular dances of the time. Here is a short bourrée (see page 68) in binary form, showing the main features of a binary-form movement:

Bear in mind The features given are generalisations; composers chose to interpret binary form in different ways, for example, there may not be a modulation at the end of Section A, or the first theme may not return in Section B.

> **Remember**
> The keyboards in general use at this time were harpsichords and clavichords. It was quite a while later that the piano became the most common domestic keyboard instrument.

Playlist: Form (Binary)

- Bach: Notebook for Anna Magdalena Bach, MInuet G Major, BWV Anh. 114
- Handel: Music for the Royal Fireworks: Suite HWV 351: II. Bourrée
- Brahms: Waltzes, Op. 39: Waltz Nr. 3 in G# Minor

During the Baroque period, it became common practice for composers to group a collection of contrasting pieces into a suite. These pieces (most often dances of different kinds) were usually in one key or in closely related keys. The first piece in a suite was sometimes a prelude, or introductory piece. It was rather informal; this style of piece originated from players checking the tuning of their instrument by improvising around a few chords in the key(s) of the suite. After all, at this time it was necessary to tune even keyboard instruments before every performance. This prelude was then followed by a number of contrasting slow and fast dances.

Other collections of dances or dance-style movements at this time were often called sonata da camera. (The word sonata means 'played [by an instrument]' and camera means 'chamber'.) Sonatas consisting of four pieces (usually arranged slow – fast – slow – fast without dance titles) were often called sonata da chiesa ('church sonatas'). These were more serious in character. Trio sonatas were sonatas written for two melody instruments and basso continuo (see page 72).

Single pieces or dances within a collection are usually called movements. Over the years it has become the custom at concerts not to applaud between movements because it prevents the audience hearing the contrasts of moods and keys in the collection of pieces.

For Grade 6 you need to know the following types of movements:

Dance movements usually written in binary form

> **Did you know?**
> The following dance movements are the most common in the Baroque suite. They often appear in the following order after a Prelude: **Allemande, Courante, Sarabande, Menuetts I and II, Gigue.**

Playlist: Dance Suite
- Bach: Lute Suite No. 1 in E Minor, BWV 996
- Bach: Cello Suite No. 3 in C Major, BWV 1009

Allemande

This is a German dance (**Allemande** is the French word for **German**) and is to be played at a moderate speed. The time signature is either $\frac{4}{4}$ or **C**. Its melody line is usually smooth and flowing and it tends to start with a short anacrusis (♪, ♫, or ♪). Dotted rhythms are sometimes used, and, if this is the case, there is a sense of grandeur and stateliness about the music. Here are the first couple of bars of two Allemandes:

🔊 116

🔊 117
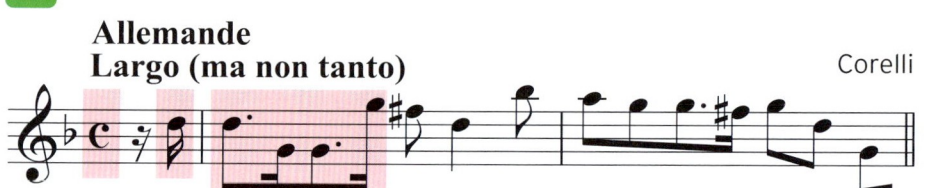

> **Handy tip!**
> The coloured boxes show some features of each dance.

Bear in mind Definitions given here are generalisations; composers chose to interpret the dances in different ways. Dance moves, speeds and the way ornaments were played differed from country to country.

Bourrée

This is a fast dance, usually in 4/4 or 2/2. It often starts with an anacrusis on the last crotchet of the bar.

Courante

The word courante means *running*. There are two main types of dance, the Italian corrente and the French courante. The use of anacrusis is common.

The Italian corrente is fast and in 3/4 or 3/8 often with continuous movement in the melody line.

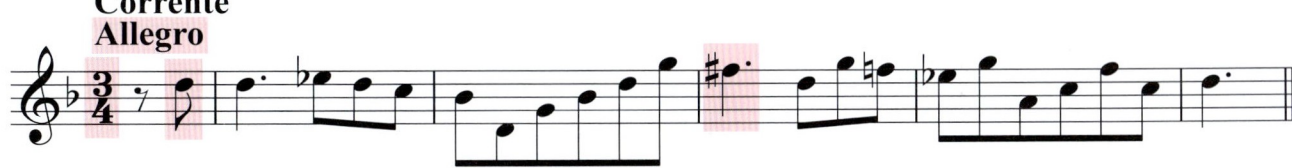

The French courante is often slower and is usually written in 3/4, 3/2 or 6/4 time. It is quite common for the French version to include hemiolas (see page 14) when approaching cadence points.

Gavotte

This dance is similar to the bourrée, though slower, usually in 2/2 or 4/4. It often has a feeling of two in a bar and tends to start with an anacrusis on the last two crotchets of the bar.

Gigue

The word is thought to come from the English dance, the **Jig**. There are two main types, the Italian **giga** and the French **gigue**. Both often feature ♩ ♪ or ♩. ♫ or ♫♩ rhythms and a short anacrusis. The Italian dance is fast and often in 12/8 time.

The French dance tends to be in either 6/8 or 12/8 and is more likely to be polyphonic in texture.

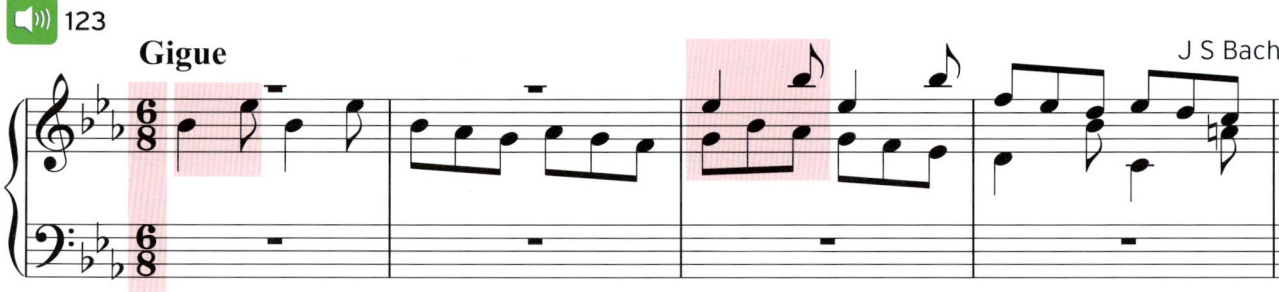

Minuet (or Menuett)

The **minuet** is a moderately paced dance, usually in 3/4, often composed in two-bar segments to fit the dance moves of the style. It normally starts on the first beat of the bar.

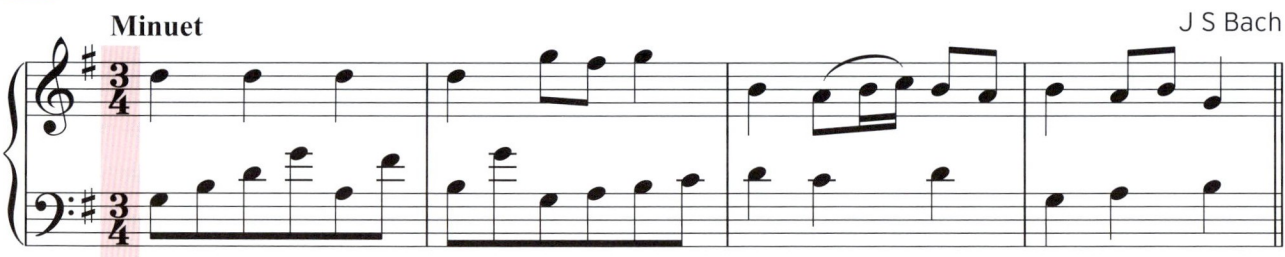

Sarabande

A slow, measured dance usually in 3/4 or 3/2, sometimes with a feeling of heaviness on the second beat. (♩ ♩. ♪ or ♩ ♩. ♩ are common). Composers rarely use an anacrusis.

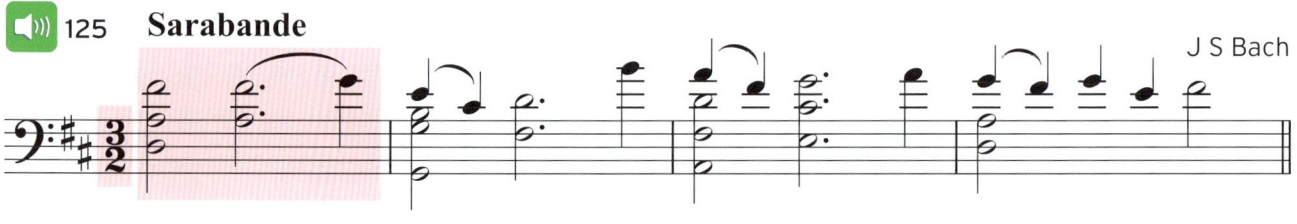

Air with variations

An **air with variations** is often used by composers who want to decorate an air (a tune with accompaniment) in different ways. The air is played first and there follow a number of other versions; in these the composer may change the rhythm, the melody, the accompaniment, the key (usually to a closely related key), the texture, the articulation and/or the dynamics. The theme is usually in binary form.

 **Playlist: Air with Variations**

- Handel: The Harmonious Blacksmith (Air and Variations in E Major from Suite No. 5, Book I)
  (Theme 0:00, Var. 1 0:52, Var. 2 1:29, Var. 3 2:06, Var. 4 2:39, Var. 5 3:13)
- Mozart: Piano Sonata No.6 in D Major, K.284 "Dürnitz" : 3:Tema Con Variazion
  (Theme 0:00, Var. 1 1:20, Var. 2 2:25, Var. 3 3:30, Var. 4 4:32, Var. 5 5:33, Var. 6 6:53,
  Var. 7 7:49, Var. 8 9:27, Var. 9 10:22, Var. 10 11:18, Var 11 12:09, Var. 12 15:47)
- Haydn: Keyboard Sonata (Divertimento) No. 7 in D Major, Hob.XVII:D1: I. Tema with Variation
  (Theme 0:00, Var. 1 0:57, Var. 2 1:55, Var. 3 2:49)
- Brahms: Variations on a theme by Haydn, Op. 56a "St. Anthony Variations": Thema, "Chorale St. Antoni"

Ternary form

Ternary form is sometimes known as ABA structure because there are three sections to it:

The first section (A) is often in binary form. Its end is marked by a perfect cadence in the tonic key. The second section (B), also often in binary form, is in a closely related key, with a contrasting melody and mood. Its end is marked by a perfect cadence in the related key.

The third section (A) is a repeat of section A.

Dances in binary form are sometimes joined together to make ternary-form movements:

Section A	Section B	Section A
Gavotte I	Gavotte II	Gavotte I
Bourrée I	Bourrée II	Bourrée I
Minuet I	Minuet II or Trio*	Minuet I

*A **trio** is a type of minuet (originally played by three players, thus the name).

 **Playlist: Ternary Form**

- Bach: Cello Suite No. 3 in C Major, BWV 1009: V. Bourrées I & II
- Lully: Gavotte
- Haydn: Sonata (Partita) in D Major, Hob. XVI:14, L. 16: II. Menuet – Trio

Other Grade 6 forms

The chorale is a type of hymn which has its origins in the German Protestant church service. The melody is often sung by the congregation with a harmonic accompaniment provided by a pipe organ or sometimes an SATB choir. Chorales are written in strophic form (the same music is used for a number of verses), though in this book the words are not included.

Quite a number of chorale melodies were written by Martin Luther and by the beginning of the Baroque period lots of chorale melodies were in circulation. Many composers liked composing different harmonisations of well-known chorale tunes. Bach's versions are particularly famous.

Playlist: Chorale

- Bach : Ach bleib bei uns, Herr Jesu Christ, BWV 253
- Bach: Allein zu dir, Herr Jesu Christ, BWV 261
- Bach: Christus, der uns selig macht, BWV 283

The folk ballad is a folk song usually written in strophic form where the words tell a story. It may also be in verse and refrain form. These ballads may be written in a key or mode.

Playlist: Folk Ballad

- Joan Baez: Henry Martin
- Shirley Collin: Barbara Allen
- Alvin Pleasant Carter, Bill Eugene Garner, Wiley Bill (Anita Carter): Wildwood Flower sung by Anita Carter

Pedal point

A pedal point is a musical word to describe music where one note (usually the tonic or dominant of the piece) is played continuously above or below chords that may or may not fit with it as a harmony note.

 126

Gavotte II ou la Musette J S Bach

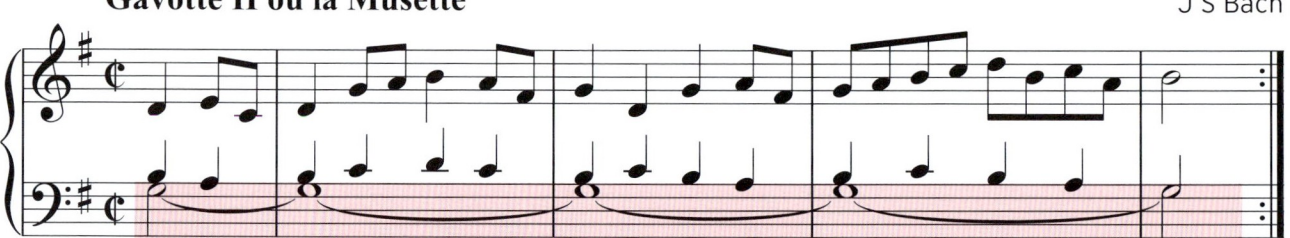

Playlist: Pedal Point

- Karl Jenkins: Palladio: I. Allegretto (tonic pedal)
- Haydn: Missa in angustiis "Nelson Mass", Hob. XXII:11 in D minor: Kyrie (0:03) (tonic pedal)
- Richard Strauss: Also sprach Zarathustra, Op. 30: I. Prelude. Sonnenaufgang (tonic pedal from opening until 1:06)
- Mozart: Piano Sonata No. 6 in D Major, K. 284 "Dürnitz": I. Allegro (dominant pedal 0:07, tonic pedal 0:14l)
- Amy Beach: Pastorale (tonic & dominant drone)
- Wagner: Die Walkure, Act III: Ride of the Valkyries (inverted dominant pedal on woodwind trill opening until 0:26)

Instrument-specific instructions

Bowed string instruments

arco – use the bow to play the music

double stopping – play the notes of the chord together (two notes); where there are three or more notes, quickly play the notes two at a time, usually from the bottom up

con sordino – put a mute onto the bridge to partially dampen the sound

natural harmonics [°] – softly touch the string at a place where a harmonic will sound

open strings [o] – play an open string

pizzicato (pizz.) – pluck the string to sound the notes, without using the bow

Playlist: Bowed Instrument Techniques

- **Arco** Mendelssohn: Violin Concerto in E Minor, Op. 64, MWV O14: II. Andante (0:39)
- **Double stopping** Bruch: Violin Concerto No. 1 in G minor, Op. 26: 3. Finale (Allegro energico (0:23)
- **Pizz.** Debussy: Sonata for Cello and Piano, L. 135: II. Sérénade
- **Open strings** Bruch: Violin Concerto No. 1 in G minor, Op. 26: 1. Vorspiel (Allegro moderato) (0:20)
- **Harmonics** Debussy: Sonata for Cello and Piano, L. 135: II. Sérénade (0:24)
- **Con sordino** (with mute) Shostakovich: Sonata for Cello and Piano in D Minor, Op. 40: I. Allegro non troppo (6:30)

Basso continuo

basso continuo – This means literally 'continuous bass'. In many Baroque pieces the composers write just a bass line below a melody (or melodies), with figures (figured bass) to show what harmonies the keyboard player (or sometimes lutenist or harpist) should use to improvise around the chord progression. This bass line was strengthened by a bass instrument (such as bassoon, cello or double bass). The combination of these instruments is called the *basso continuo*, or in its abbreviated form, *continuo*.

Analysis

1. Look at the following movement and answer the questions on page 75.

1. In which key is this movement? _____

2. To which related key has this movement modulated by the end of section A? _____

3. Name two keys through which the music travels back to the tonic in section B. _____
   _____
   _____

4. In which bars are there both harmonic and melodic sequences in the same bar? _____

5. In which bars is there a pedal point on the tonic of the relative major key? _____

6. What cadence finishes the movement? _____

7. On what note should you start the trill in bar 24 (violin part)? _____

8. Bracket (⌐▔▔▔) a one-octave scale starting and finishing on the supertonic (violin part).

9. Name the interval between the two notes marked with asterisks (*) in bar 9 (violin part). _____
   _____

10. Comment on the pitch in the first beat of bar 17 (violin part). _____
    _____

11. Name the note(s) that are unaccented passing notes in the first two beats of bar 1 (violin part). _____

12. Name a bar where there is an example of syncopation (violin part). _____

13. Compare the rhythm of the violin melody with the harmonic rhythm in bar 1 of this movement. _____
    _____

14. Name two bars where there are three descending notes of a chromatic scale (violin part). _____

15. Name the note values of the second fastest notes in this movement. _____
    _____

2 Look at the following movement and answer the questions below.

1. Name two features that make this movement typical of a Minuet. _____
   _____

2. In which key is this movement? _____

3. To which related key has this movement modulated by bar 8? _____

4. Circle the first accidental that signals this modulation.

5. Name the key through which the music travels back to the tonic in section B. _____

6. Circle the first accidental that signals the modulation back to the tonic in section B.

7. What cadence finishes the movement? _____

8. What is the name of the ornament to be played at bar 11? _____

9. Describe how a musician should play the ornament at bar 11. _____
   _____

10. In how many individual parts is this movement written? _____

11. Name the interval between the two notes marked with asterisks (*) in bars 14-15 (treble part). _____

12. In which bar is there the same type of interval as marked with asterisks (*) in bars 14-15 (treble part)?
    _____

13. Comment on the pitch of the notes in bar 1 (bass line). _____
    _____

14. Name the accented passing note in bar 1 (treble part). _____

15. Compare the pitch of the melody in bar 1 with that of bar 10 (treble part). _____

3 Look at the following movement and answer the questions on page 79.

1. Write down a rhythmic feature from this movement which is typical of a Sarabande.
   _____
   _____
   _____

2. At what tempo should a musician play this movement? _____

3. In which key is this movement? _____

4. Write the last chord of section A as a chord symbol. _____

5. What cadence finishes the movement? _____

6. In which bars of section B are there both harmonic and melodic sequences in the same bar? _____
   _____

7. Name the bars where there is a perfect cadence in B minor in section B. _____

8. Name two keys through which the music travels back to the tonic in section B after bar 17. _____
   _____

9. Comment on the harmonic rhythm in bars 9-12. _____
   _____

10. Describe the rhythm and melodic shape of this movement (bass line). _____
    _____
    _____

11. Name two bars where there is a lower chromatic auxiliary note (continuo part). _____

12. Circle two examples of an interval of an augmented 4th (violin part).

13. Name the interval that begins most of the phrases (violin part). _____

14. Compare the pitch of the melody in bars 14-16 with bars 22-24 (violin part). _____
    _____

15. Give a reason why it would be difficult for a flautist to play this movement. _____
    _____

Theory of Music Grade 6
Sample Paper

Your full name (as on appointment form). Please use BLOCK CAPITALS.

_____

Your signature   Candidate ID

_____   _____

Centre

_____

Instructions to Candidates

1. The time allowed for answering this paper is **three (3) hours**.
2. Fill in your name and the candidate number printed on your appointment form in the appropriate spaces on this paper, and on any other sheets that you use.
3. **Do not open this paper until you are told to do so.**
4. This paper contains **seven (7) sections** and you should answer all of them.
5. Read each question carefully before answering it. Your answers must be written legibly in pen or pencil in the spaces provided.
6. You are reminded that you are bound by the regulations for written exams displayed at the exam centre and listed on page 4 of the current edition of the written exams syllabus. In particular, you are reminded that you are not allowed to bring books, music or papers into the exam room. Bags must be left at the back of the room under the supervision of the invigilator.
7. If you leave the exam room you will not be allowed to return.

Examiner's use only:

1 (10)	
2 (15)	
3 (15)	
4 (15)	
5 (10)	
6 (15)	
7 (20)	
Total	

Sample Paper   Grade 6

Section 1 (10 marks)

Boxes for examiner's use only

1.1   Which minor key has this key signature?

   Key _____

1.2   What is the relative major key of C sharp minor? _____

1.3   What does the interval of a minor 7th become when inverted? _____

1.4   Add the correct time signature to this bar.

1.5   Name a major key in which this interval is found.

   Key _____

1.6   Which note is the leading note of the minor key with a key signature of five sharps?

   _____

1.7   Write the correct chord symbol above this triad.

1.8   Write the correct figured bass indication below this chord.

81

1.9 What is the key of this passage?

Key _____

1.10 Give the meaning of **pizz.** _____

Section 2 (15 marks)

2.1 Add accidentals to the notes which need them to make this a descending scale of B♭ melodic minor.

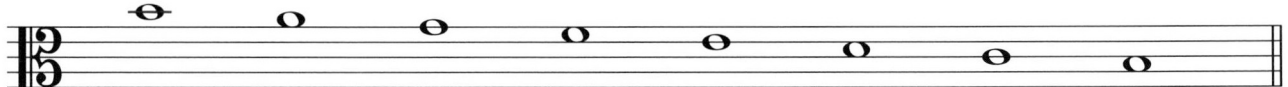

2.2 Write, in four groups of four quavers, an ascending broken chord of the diminished seventh on E. Do not use a key signature but add accidentals as needed.

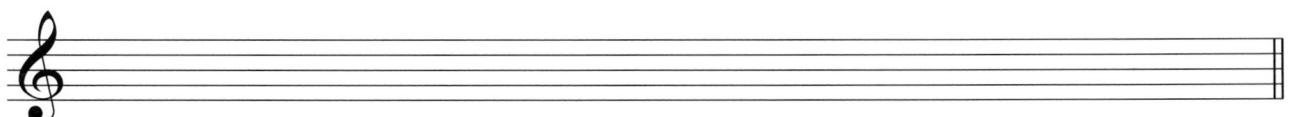

2.3 This passage is written for clarinet in B flat. Re-write it at sounding pitch, using the correct key signature.

Sample Paper   Grade 6

Section 3 (15 marks)

3.1 Write an 8-bar melody for oboe in the key of G major. You may use the following as a start if you wish:

Section 4 (15 marks)

4.1 Continue this chord progression by writing it one step higher at each repetition to form a harmonic sequence, ending as shown:

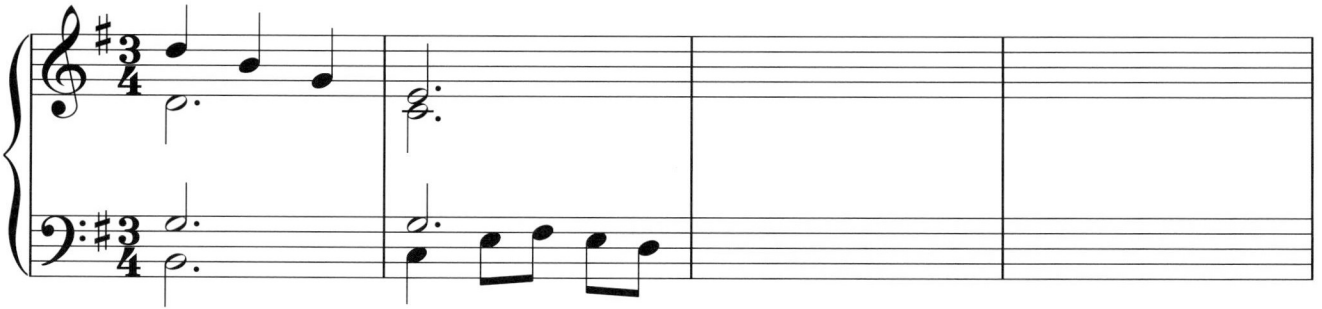

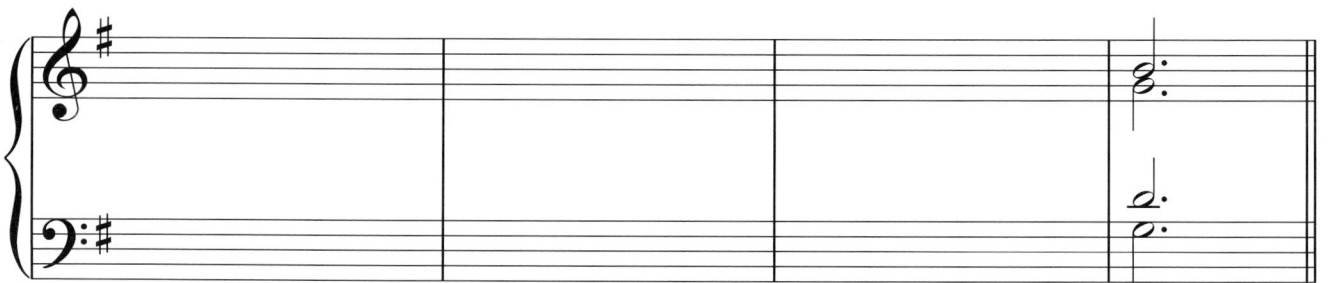

Section 5 (10 marks)

5.1 Write out this passage in close score.

J S Bach

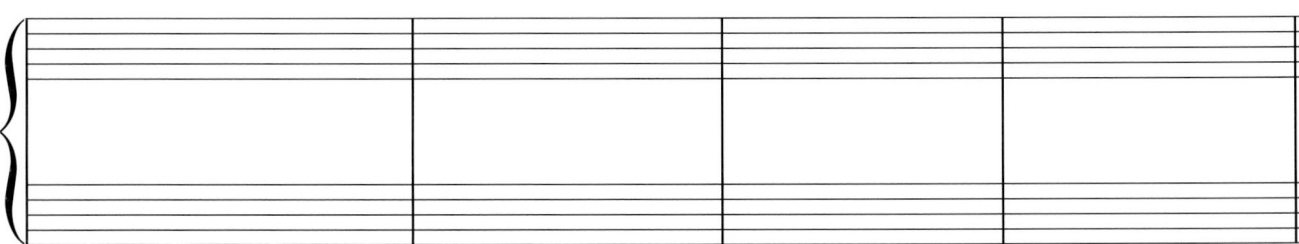

Section 6 (15 marks)

6.1 Label the chords of this phrase with Roman numerals below the stave and chord symbols above, and complete it with an appropriate cadence.

Sample Paper

Grade 6

Section 7 (20 marks)

Study this passage and answer the questions on the following page.

J S Bach

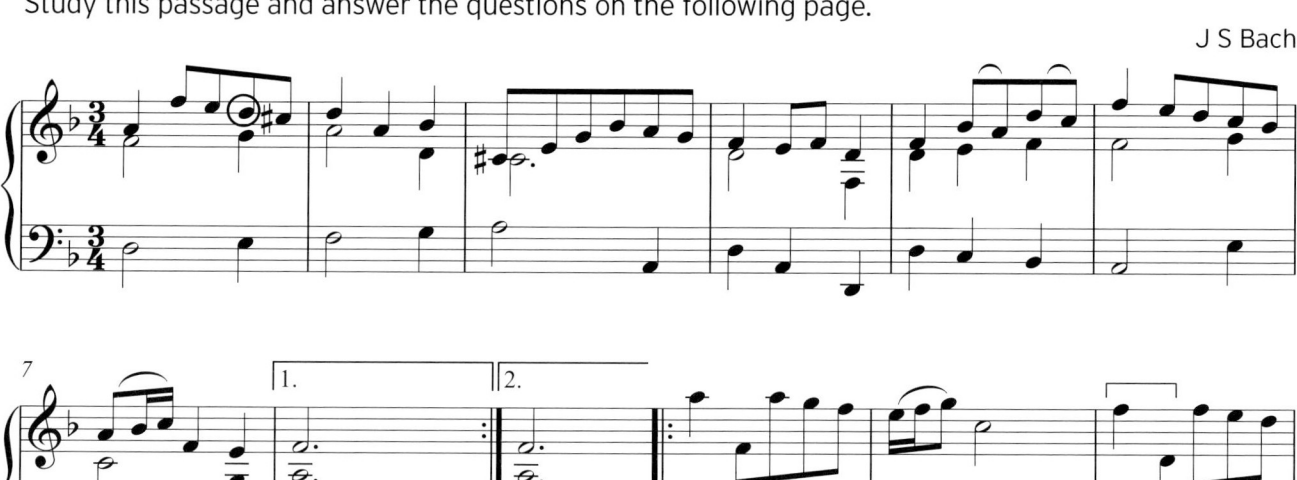

85

Sample Paper Grade 6

7.1 What is the tonic key? _____

7.2 In what key is the cadence at bar 7 (third beat) to bar 8? _____

7.3 What is the name of the cadence at bar 15 (third beat) to 16? _____

7.4 Write the correct chord symbol above the second chord of bar 15.

7.5 Write the correct Roman numeral below the first beat of bar 14.

7.6 Write the correct figured bass indication below the chord on the third beat of bar 6.

7.7 What kind of note (eg auxiliary note) is the final note in bar 3 (upper line)?
_____

7.8 What kind of chord (eg dominant 7th) is formed by the first four notes in the upper line of bar 3?
_____

7.9 Name the interval between the first two notes (bracketed) in the upper line of bar 11.
_____

7.10 How would you describe the circled note in bar 1 (eg auxiliary note)? _____

Instrument ranges

The ranges given here are the written ranges for players of approximately Grade 8 standard. The complete ranges (especially for string instruments) go higher. **You need to memorise the transposing intervals for the instruments in the coloured boxes.**

Woodwind instruments

Flute		
Descant recorder		sounds an octave higher
Treble recorder		
Oboe		
Clarinet in B flat		sounds a major 2nd lower
Clarinet in A		sounds a minor 3rd lower
Bassoon		
Soprano saxophone in B flat		sounds a major 2nd lower
Alto saxophone in E flat		sounds a major 6th lower
Tenor saxophone in B flat		sounds a major 9th lower
Baritone saxophone in E flat		sounds a compound major 6th lower

Brass instruments

Trumpet in B flat		sounds a major 2nd lower
French horn in F		sounds a perfect 5th lower

String instruments

Violin		
Viola		
Cello		
Double bass		sounds an octave lower
Classical guitar		sounds an octave lower

Voice ranges

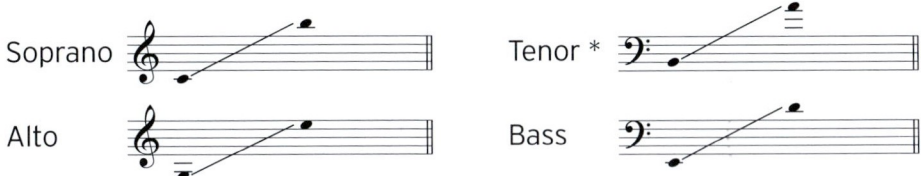

* In open score, music for tenor voice is almost always written in treble clef an octave higher than it sounds

Different words – same meaning

In music there are often different words to describe the same thing. You need to know the following for Grade 6:

Aeolian mode – natural minor
basso continuo – continuo
C+ (in relation to chord symbols) – Caug
C°7 – Cdim7
close score – short score, 'piano' score, reduced score
copy (in relation to melody lines or harmony) – imitate
duple time – two beats in a bar
homophonic – block chords
improvise (improvisatory) – jamming, extemporise, make up music (often based on a particular chord progression)
leading note – te (major keys only)
mediant – me (major keys only)
open score – full score
pedal bass – pedal point, drone bass
polyphonic – contrapuntal
quadruple time – four beats in a bar
submediant – la (major keys only)
theme – subject, idée fixe, air, theme tune (film and TV music)
triple time – three beats in a bar

English and Italian words for instruments

Wind instruments
recorder – flauto dolce
flute – flauto
oboe – oboe
bassoon – fagotto

String instruments
violin – violino
viola – viola
cello – violoncello
double bass – contrabasso

Brass instruments
trumpet – tromba
horn – corno

Percussion instruments
harpsichord – clavicembalo
kettle drum – timpani

Remember
You may use American terms in your exam, but there is no need to use them at all if you do not want to.